# HEALING CURRENT

## A Plug Into The Power Of God

## C.M.D LAMAI

## Healing Current  By C.M-D Lamai

Published by:

Stay Alive Int'l
Beseech Concept Suite: 11, Olowu Street, Ikeja, Lagos
stayaliveintl@gmail.com
+234 809 822 0369, 802 930 9859


C.M-D Lamai
E-mail: cmdlamai@gmail.com
ndamarvel@yahoo.com
cottagechristian@yahoo.com
AFRICA: +234 80515 333 43
U.K: +44 79564 11752
USA: +190 1236 1659

Unless otherwise stated all scripture references are from the Holy Bible,
King James Version and New Living Translation.

# ACKNOWLEDGEMENTS

The **GOSPEL** is a **TRUST**.
**LORD**, I am still grateful for the opportunity entrusted me to preach this gospel that is liberating lives across Nations.

# TABLE OF CONTENT

# CHAPTER 1
# IN THE BEGINNING.

*A*bout a year before my grandfather went to be with the Lord, I had the privilege of sitting with him for hours while he narrated his life story to me.

He was tall and handsome and had a good command of the English language. He was one of the first few educated Nigerians who learnt the language on first hand basis from our colonial masters.

Grandpa, Chief A.A Lamai became the first man to own a car, own a gramophone and build a modern house in my home town which was popularly called the Kukuruku Hills because of its topography which was a defense barricade for the people during the inter-tribal wars and the historical Nupe invasion. Grandpa was considered a successful man in his day yet he said to me, "Son, I regret the life I have lived" when I asked why? He said, "I was supposed to be a priest but my parents refused because I was the only son they had" He also told me how much he desired for one of his children to become a priest when he realized he couldn't fulfill the call, but none took that path.

By this time, I was already a Seminarian and that was the reason he sent for me. My Dad told him I was being trained to be a priest. He sat me down for hours telling me several stories and the summary of it all was that he had a call from God to be a priest which he never fulfilled but believed that the call upon his life had been transferred to me and that whatever I do, I must not fail God like he did.

That was the moment I began to place some value on the call of God upon my life knowing that I was privileged to receive what someone else lost. Though, I didn't fully understand it and I think I still don't but I know better now.

I have heard stories of people who started out by hearing a voice or seeing a vision but none of that happened to me at the beginning. I started out with a strong desire to live for others. I just wanted to be there for those who needed help beyond themselves. I was eleven years old when my dad asked what I would like to become in future in order for him to determine what school I should attend after my primary education. I told him I wanted to either become a soldier or a priest. All I had in mind was to live my life helping others, but what I didn't know was that God was pulling me through my desires towards the call.

I ended up with the latter and became a Seminarian for six years at St Paul's Catholic Seminary, Benin City under the tutelage of the great Rev. Fr Stephen Ogbeide whom I still consider as one of the greatest men of God I have ever met.

He became my mentor. He specifically taught me among many other things; discipline, reverence for God and for the things of God, accountability in everything even to the minutest detail. He taught me ethics in ministry and in life generally, he taught me dignity in labor and how to magnify my office. Even if I leave out any other thing, I wouldn't leave this one thing out - He taught me diction to the extent that he would even flog me when I pronounced words wrongly especially the ones he expected me to know. I didn't like it then, but looking back now, I will be eternally grateful for his input in my life and ministry.

At that time, I was more religious than spiritual but right now, I am more spiritual than religious and because of my spirituality through personal encounters with God.

I now appreciate the foundation of my religious disciplines. I know when to stand and fight and when to run from appearances of evil. I know how to behave when I'm with kings and when I'm with paupers. I know how to be with God and how to be with people. I know when it's time to speak up and when it's time to be silent.

All these and more are the foundation for carrying and maintaining the power of God. Unfortunately, this is lacking among many of today's believers and ministers of the gospel. Very few people are willing to be mentored, trained and disciplined the right way. Most times, we submit to authority as long as it fits our mould but there is nothing like a convenient submission. It just doesn't exist. It would take the power of God to raise you up but it would take both the power of God and your own judicious and religious discipline to stay up. I have seen and heard stories of many who were once up but fell and couldn't rise anymore because they were not prepared to maintain such levels of authority.

Today, I see the healing and miracle power of God manifest in my life every time a demand is placed on it. That didn't happen overnight. In this book, I want to try to tell you about the **HEALING CURRENT** of God.

What it's all about, who can have and enjoy it, how to generate it, how to maintain it, how to disburse it and how to enjoy it.

# THE INJECTION

I was a sickly baby, always being rushed from hospital to hospital. One day, I fell sick and was taken to a Baptist hospital in Shaki, Oyo State, where a nurse accidentally broke a needle inside my body, specifically, at my right backside, while administering an injection to me, and for fear of losing her job, told no one about it and acted as if all was well. As a result, my body began to swell and smell. I was moved from hospital to hospital with no solution in view because the situation could not be diagnosed. It was only a matter of time before they eventually decoded the source of the problem as it was traced to a broken piece of needle at my backside.

According to medical advice, if I would survive, an operation had to be done to get the puss out of my body and my right leg had to be amputated. At that juncture, my parents had to make a decision. As God would do it, my Dad refused and decided he would rather have me dead than leave me crippled for the rest of my life. He refused to sign up for amputation. My parents decided to pray about it and leave it in the hands of God. As soon as they travelled back home with me from Oyo State to Edo State, it only took three days of absolute dependence on the healing power of God and I was supernaturally healed and totally restored.

That I am not just alive today, but I am well and walking with both legs in perfect form and shape, I owe it to the grace of God and to my parents who were sensitive to the plan of God and cooperated with his power. I believe this to be my major assignment on earth, which is to preach Jesus Christ by manifesting the power of God in healing the sick and working supernatural miracles, signs and wonders. I believe I had to experience that power so I can bring others into that experience.

John says it this way, *"That which was from the beginning, which we have heard, which we have seen with our eyes, which we looked upon and have touched with our hands (experienced) concerning the word of life - 2 the life was made manifest and we have seen it and testify to it and proclaim to you the eternal life which was with the father and was manifest to us. - 3 that which we have seen and heard we proclaim also to you, so that you too may have fellowship with us; and indeed our fellowship is with the Father and with his Son Jesus Christ. - 4 and we are writing these things so that our joy may be complete 1 John 1:1-4".*

**"** Its amazing how God can birth our ministries out of our miseries. God doesnt have waste products. **"**

With God everything and every area of your life can be positively productive including the issues and experiences you are ashamed of.

**"** Whatever is put in Gods hands will eventually make sense. As a matter of fact, the power of God leaks out of the broken places of our lives. **"**

# THE CALL

## THE JOURNEY

So many years ago, when I started what I would call my first church in Lagos, things were going good until we suddenly were asked to quit our place of worship without adequate notice. Nowadays things are getting better in Lagos compared to those days when a property owner could decide all of a sudden to do what he liked, when and how he liked and no one would be able to challenge him. I wouldn't say the system has completely changed now, but at least, it's getting better.

That incident affected the church so much that our membership reduced drastically because we had to be meeting under a shed for about a year before we eventually got another place. It was during those days, that a minister of God said to me, "Are you sure God called you? ...Because you should not be going through this if He did." I must confess, I felt like punching him in the face but thank God my hands were already nailed to the cross. This was someone who had never pioneered anything.

13

He was just an employee of a large ministry and doesn't have a clue what the founders must have gone through.

Oftentimes, people who have become successful at whatever they do, don't tell us the truth about how they arrived at their achievements. They tell us their stories but keep back the parts we really need. This is the reason so many people give up in their pursuits because they have not been told the whole truth about how to arrive at success.

In ministry especially, we have been brain washed to believe that if God sent you everything would always fall in place for you, and if it doesn't, then something is wrong with you or with the vision, so that when you fail, there's always the tendency to quit because you probably must have missed God somewhere. The devil is a liar! God knew you would not be able to catch all the lessons all at once, so He made available, grace to help in time of need. Friend, there would always be a time of need and then a time of plenty.

There's life after a mishap, there's life after a fall, in business, ministry, professional career, just name it.

There is room for growth in God's agenda for your life.

The bible says, the righteous falls several times but he'll never be defeated. His righteousness will not allow him to stay down; he'll rise again and again. Righteousness is a spring-board. It is a lifter, for righteousness exalts a nation. If it can raise up an entire nation then it can definitely raise an individual. Glory to God; we are the righteousness of God in Christ Jesus. We have been declared undefeatable!

I want to let you know you are not out of place when you are confronted with the challenges of life. People may not tell you how and what they fought to get where they are, they may not tell you how their marriages almost failed, they may not tell you how they did menial jobs to pay their bills, they may never tell you how many failed attempts they had experienced before they finally made a headway. My dear, you'd have to cross over by the grace of God. The pathway of pain is a path in the growth process. Knowledge grows, wisdom grows and power also grows on the soil of painful experiences. Dont give up on your calling. God can't work with discouraged servants. Stay motivated.

The degree of your past or present struggle is an index to the magnanimity of your future glory. God would refurbish what people would throw away.

" And we know that God causes everything to work together for the good of those who love God and are called according to his purpose for them. "Rom. 8:28 (NLT).

God doesn't want your painful experiences to be wasted.

# THE HEALING MINISTRY

"For since the creation of the world God's invisible qualities—his eternal power and divine nature—have been clearly seen, being understood from what has been made, so that people are without excuse." Romans 1:20 (NIV)

The healing ministry is an amazing ministry. It operates in two dimensions. There is the natural dimension and the supernatural dimension.

The natural dimension is the realm where healing happens through natural and scientific treatments. The human body has been created to heal itself naturally, ceteris paribus (all things being equal). This is the reason why a minor injury can be healed without applying any form of treatment. In this realm, we can also be healed through the application of natural herbs.

*"And God said, Behold, I have given you every herb bearing seed, which is upon the face of all the earth, and every tree in which is the fruit of a tree yielding seed; to you it shall be for meat. "Gen 1:29.*

*"He causeth the grass to grow for the cattle, and herb for the service of man… Psalms 104:14. "For one believeth that he may eat all things: Another, who is weak (sick), eateth herbs" Rom 14:2.*

*"And by the river upon the bank thereof, on this side and on that side, shall grow all trees for meat, whose leaf shall not fade, neither shall the fruit thereof be consumed; it shall bring forth new fruits according to his months, because their matters they issued out of the sanctuary; and the fruit thereof shall be for meat and the leaf thereof for medicine:" Ezekiel 47:12.*

God has made provision for us to be healed through herbal treatments Revelation 22:2.

# SCIENTIFIC MEDICATION

**JEREMIAH 8:22** "Is there no balm (medication) in Gilead? Is there no physician (medical doctor) there? Why then is there no healing for the wound of my people?"

**3 JOHN 1:2** "Beloved, I wish above all things that thou mayest prosper and be in health, even as thy soul prospereth."

Apart from the other two provisions earlier discussed, there is also a third provision for healing in the natural dimension and it is healing through medical science. Some people don't believe in medical science, but I do. One of the outstanding and unique qualitity of God is His Omniscience...................................................................
..............................
I believe God made provision for everybody at every level. I believe that medical science is God's way of administering his healing power in the natural realm to reach everybody at their levels until they can come up to his level -The supernatural faith level.

Science is the intellectual and practical activity encompassing the systematic study of the structure and behavior of the physical and natural world through observation and experiment. Science simply means, particular knowledge, and in Hosea 4:6, the word of God says, *"My people are destroyed for lack of knowledge. Knowledge is power - Power to make things happen. It is not just power, it is the power of God to help man live a great and abundant life.*

Genesis 1:1 tells us, *"In the beginning, God created the heaven (spiritual) and the earth (natural)."* In other words, God is the source of both the spiritual and the natural realms. This means God is behind medical healing as much as he is behind supernatural or faith healings.
*"Behold, I will bring it health and cure, and I will cure them and I will reveal unto them the abundance of peace and truth."Jeremiah 33:6.*

# SUPERNATURAL HEALINGS
## I COR 12: 8-10

For to one is given by the Spirit the Word of Wisdom; to another the Word of Knowledge by the same Spirit;
To another Faith by the same Spirit; to another the Gifts of healing by the same Spirit;
To another the Working of miracles; to another Prophecy; to another Discerning of spirits; to another Divers kinds of tongues; to another the Interpretation of tongues:

Supernatural healing is that which happens only through the administration of faith. Hence, people call it faith healing.
In this realm anything is possible because it is in the God realm. All other provisions for healing earlier discussed are the power of God in operation but only this happens in the spirit realm where nothing is impossible.

In this case, the levels of our faith can determine the degree of divine manifestations we see. However, there are so many other elements that can either enhance or slow down our results. Elements like divine will, divine training, divine gifting and callings, ignorance and so many others, to name but a few.

This realm of healing by faith is a higher realm than the natural realm of healing because in this realm, there is nothing like incurable disease. The woman with the issue of blood spent her money tarrying to get help from physicians which never happened until she turned to the supernatural dimension by releasing her faith towards the healing current flowing through the clothes of Jesus of Nazareth.

The supernatural realm doesn't know impossibilities however, with medical science, your healing always manifests through a process of time. Sometimes it would take days, weeks, months or even years to see a complete change in situation but with faith, healing may and may not require any process. It can fully manifest in a matter of minutes or even seconds.

For instance, a woman in the UK who was given about four years to go through a healing process before she could walk again due to a car accident she had that left her paralyzed on a wheelchair, was brought to me for prayers and to the amazement of all in the room, after about three minutes exhortation to stir up her faith in the supernatural, I laid hands on her and commanded her to rise up and walk and she did. It was immediate.

Glory to God! She didn't have to wait for four years anymore. As a matter of fact, I prayed for a young man in Kogi state, whom doctors have told would never walk again and he started walking immediately after prayers. How do you explain that?

We have not seen the last of this. The supernatural will keep violating the laws of the natural because the supernatural is superior to the natural. When the power of God shrinks time, it's called a miracle!

We have a beautiful couple in our church, Mr. and Mrs. Solaja who were trusting God for the fruit of the womb. They had tried several medical treatments for solution until even the doctors advised them to stop taking medication to avoid destroying the woman's womb or causing further complication. Medical science gave up at that point.

However, in one of our services, I called both of them out by the operation of the gift of the Word of knowledge. I said to the woman, "You have a brother called Chris" She said, "yes sir."

"...He lives in Kaduna in a place called Barnawa" At this point, she was overwhelmed and fell under the anointing. I asked for her to be brought back up and continued with more words of knowledge by the Spirit. I called out the date she got married, the place and the house address of where she lodged which happened to be the house address of Mr. Chris, her elder brother.

I further told her a vision I saw of how her womb was manipulated by a witch who squeezed a fruit at the wedding ceremony and swore that she would never produce any fruit from her womb that would live. Then I prophesied that she was going to have a child. Guess what? The next week, the husband called me and said, "Pastor, we just returned from the hospital, my doctor has just confirmed that my wife is one week pregnant." As I write this, they have a bouncing baby boy.

I couldn't make it to the naming ceremony but two of our pastors did on my behalf and they told me he was named, Peniel. Glory! Peniel means, *"I have seen God face to face and my life is preserved"*. *Gen 32:30*. Baby Peniel is living evidence that the supernatural power of God is real.

It doesn't matter if it's a disease, a broken bone, a missing body part, a dead organ, a defect in the body system or a demonic influence, with faith administration, a long process may not be required. God can either bypass time, shrink time or manipulate time to bring about a miracle

# CHAPTER 2

# ELECTRIC CURRENT

There are two dimensions of life - The heavenly and the earthly dimensions. The former happens in the eternal realm while the latter happens on time zone. One is spiritual and the other is natural. In Genesis 1:1 "In the beginning, God created the heaven and the earth", here, we see the origin of both of them. It is clearly stated that God is the source of the heavenly life as well as the earthly life. He is the source of both the spiritual and the natural worlds – spiritual power and natural power.

The earthly is an inferior replica of the heavenly and that is because unlike the earthly, the heavenly is indestructible. It is flawless and eternal whereas the earthly is full of flaws and subject to corruption.

However, the things we see on earth were fashioned and patterned after heavenly realities including man who was himself fashioned after the image and likeness of God, only clothed with inferior material (flesh) to enable his functionality here on earth, whereas God is encircled in light and is declared to be a Spirit.

*"Praise the Lord, my soul. Lord my God, you are very great; you are clothed with splendour and majesty. The Lord wraps himself in light as with a garment; he stretches out the heavens like a tent."* (NIV) *Ps 104:1-2.*

One day, I had a vision where I was ministering to a large crowd while stretching forth my hands and all of a sudden, I saw blue flames coming out of my hands and flowing towards the people and as it touched them, they were all overwhelmed with different reactions. Some shouted, some cried aloud, and others very softly, some fell to the floor and for so many others, their bodies began to vibrate just the way it happens when people get electrocuted. At that time, I didn't know what it meant until The Lord began to teach me about His healing current and how to operate it.

The Lord explained to me that the blue flame I saw was his healing current potent enough to heal every disease but that the degree of result I would see in my ministry, would be dependent on the amount of voltage I can generate, carry and manage. He said to me, "some can generate it but can't carry the weight for long, while others can carry it but don't know how to utilize, appropriate or manage it.

The Lord showed me a scripture I had never seen before in the book of Proverbs chapter 20, verse 30 and it reads,

"The blueness of a wound cleanseth away evil: so *do* stripes the inward parts of the belly."

When the **BLUENESS** of God rests upon a wound, a sickness or a situation, it immediately attacks the evil and that spiritual power that deals with evil is compared to a natural way of getting rid of character flaws by applying a physical force or discipline. The blue flame functions like electric current.

Electricity is the most important invention of all time. Greeks first found out around 600 BC that rubbing amber and fur together caused static electricity. For many years electricity was a mystery and many inventors experimented in order to understand more about how electricity works and how it could be used.

There were many people that contributed to the invention of electricity. Among those are William Gilbert, Francis Hauksbee,

Benjamin Franklin, Luigi Galvani, and more. On October 17th, 1831, Michael Faraday demonstrated that passing a magnet through a coil of wire could produce electricity.

This was the documented time of invention and Faraday just happened to be the right mind in the right place at the right time.

There were many obstacles during the invention of electricity. Problems occurred frequently and the steps to understanding how it worked were very slow. The real key to how electricity progressed is the way the inventors fed off of each other's revelations.

As one man would question something another would start to prove him wrong. This happened for many years. An example occurred in 1786 when Galvani experimented with a frog and electrical current. He found that a discharge of static made the frog's legs jerk. He claimed that the fluids in the leg supplied electricity but Alessandro Volta did not agree.

Volta built the voltaic pile, an early type of battery, to prove the electrical charge came from the battery.

As electricity developed over the years many inventions followed. The battery followed. Volta invented an early type of battery and the current from the battery led to Ohm's Law, which related current, voltage, and resistance. Another very important invention was the actual generation of the electricity. Once scientists knew electricity existed they worked to find a way to use it. In 1819 Hans Christian Oersted discovered that a magnetic field surrounds an electric wire. This was the beginning of breakthrough with understanding the electric current.

# TWO DIMENSIONS OF DIVINE CURRENTS

Let's examine some basic principles of electricity as they relate to the functionality of God's healing power.

If the natural things, according to the word of God, will give us a clue to how spiritual things are configured then its only wise that we compare the natural power of God which is electricity to the spiritual power of God, which is the anointing, and in this case specifically - The anointing to work miracles and heal the sick.

Electric current has its source in PROTONS, NEUTRONS AND ELECTRONS. Protons carry positive charges; Neutrons carry no charge while Electrons carry negative charges. However, the same way the electric current is traceable to these three sources, so the spiritual power of God to heal the sick is traceable to three sources. The healing power of God flows in the spirit like electricity flows in the natural.

# THE ELECTRIC SWITCH'

The word-SWITCH, as a noun, means, a device for making and breaking the connection in an electric circuit. As a verb, it means to change the position, direction, or focus of something. When you turn on a switch, you make a connection with electric power or you focus on a certain direction that releases a power flow. This same principle works with the healing power of God. You can turn it on and off at will. We have been told that the healing power of God flows as the spirit of God wills but I make bold to say it's an erroneous belief. The gift of healing is given as The Spirit wills but the use of the gift is as the gifted wills. The healing current flows when demands are placed on it by turning on the switch that is already connected to power. The switch that turns on the power of God in the Spirit realm is called desire or intention.

One day, our Lord Jesus visited a particular town where a woman who suffered from haemorrhage (an abnormal flow of blood) for twelve years lived. She did all she knew to do in order to get her healing naturally, but all to no avail, instead, her situation got worse as days went by.

Somehow, she heard that our Lord was in town and that he could heal the sick by supernatural means so she did something I want us to take note of. I'm not too sure whether she knew what she was doing as at the time she did it, but I know and understand what she did and I also know that what she did worked for her and still works today.

First of all, the sick woman said to herself... She didn't say to God and God didn't say to her. She said to herself, "if I touch the hem of his garment, I shall be made whole." This is called INTENTION. It is the switch that turned on the spiritual power of God on her behalf.

**Intention or desire is the switch that turns on or turns off the flow of the healing current of God.**

You will also notice that our Lord had to stop to find out who it was that withdrew power from him which only meant that it wasn't only by the will of the Spirit that the miracle happened but also because of the woman's intentionality. Demand was placed on the power that was already flowing because somebody turned it on.

So many people were touching the master like she did, but none of them got a miracle and the reason is simple - INTENTION! Their intentions were different. Whereas they were touching a celebrity, she was drawing on power for change.

Touching the Lord is like plugging your device into power, but the power doesn't flow just because you plugged into it, you must have to turn on the switch, which is intention or desire. Only the woman who turned on the switch enjoyed the flow of the healing current which our Lord Jesus described as virtue (current) flowing out of him. (Mark 5:25-34)

As a man of God, I can decide to turn on and turn off the power of God at will just by intending to. I can shake hands with you, this minute and nothing would happen and I can also shake hands with you the next minute and something would happen if I do it with an intention to direct the flow of God's power towards you.

There may not always be a physical reaction or manifestation, but something would always happen in the spirit.

A very dramatic incident happened in John 18:6, According to the Orthodox Jewish Bible Translation, when the soldiers came for our Lord Jesus, in revealing himself, he said to them "I am he; they recoiled and fell to the ground" I am interested in the word recoil. It means a kickback. It also means a sudden spring or flinch back in horror. I believe Jesus responded with an intention to convince them he was the true Jesus they were looking for, so they wouldn't hurt anyone else. As a matter of fact, he further made a plea for them to let the disciples go, since he was their target. The power flow was so strong it kicked back the soldiers and swept them off their feet. These were not children, not women and definitely, not weaklings. These were soldiers. The power of God can be very forceful!

*"How forcible are right words! But what doth your arguing reprove?* Job 6:25,

*" For the word of God is living and active and sharper than any two-edged sword, and piercing as far as the division of soul and spirit, of both joints and marrow, and able to judge the thoughts and intentions of the heart. 13 And there is no creature hidden from His sight, but all things are open and laid bare to the eyes of Him with whom we have to do.* Heb.4:12.

This manifestation had nothing to do with the faith of the soldiers because they had no faith in our Lord Jesus Christ. It had everything to do with the intentions of Jesus Christ, and because he wanted them to be able to arrest him, he allowed them to, by turning off the switch, otherwise; none of them would have been able to touch him and still remain on their feet. From that moment onwards, he had other conversations with them but they never felt the power, never were forced backwards and never fell to the floor again.

I remember a similar incident that happened in 2008. I was with a friend at his home in the United Kingdom, while he lamented to me about his challenge in securing a certain facility in Stratford, London.

They wanted so dearly, a certain facility for their weekly church services there and because the young man in charge of the facility didn't believe in God and didn't want a church using that facility, he decided to make things difficult for them. He narrated how he had made several attempts to pacify this young man and to get him to accept the church even at a very exorbitant prize, but the young man wouldn't just go along with it.

At that point, I said to him, "let's go to him right now!" And I further said, "get every document you would need if you were going to seal a deal because that's exactly what would happen when we meet him today." Timi laughed and said, "Lamai, you don't understand, this guy is difficult, there's nothing I haven't done." I said to him, "There's something you haven't done, just pack your things and lead me there. "To summarize it, we went. On getting there, my friend pointed out a young man in his thirties, a white guy of about 6feet tall, a Briton I suppose, wearing a hairstyle blown upwards and looked like a body builder with very broad shoulders and didn't look like he had smiled in two years.

Nevertheless, I went there with an intention. As we stood before him, I greeted him with a smile which he didn't return, even though he responded to my greeting with a nod and a British hi. I took it further anyway and stretched forth my hands for a handshake with an intention to turn on the power. That was it! Just like an electric shock there was a reaction. The power flowed through his body and he staggered backwards, but for the wall on which he leaned that held him up, he would have fallen to the ground.

For me, that was enough, just to see the shock on his face after he regained his balance. Then he asked, "What was that?" "And I said that was the power of God, I am a man of God and we would like to use this facility for church worship services" And here's the good news, he didn't just give it, he gave it to us free of charge for the first four months and gave himself too for service in the church. He became a very devoted member of the church, he became the church janitor. What an introduction! My God! What power we have! It may not always be dramatic, but something always happens, when the gift of God is intentionally released. The spiritual power of God works for those who understand it, like electricity works in the natural.

# CHAPTER 3

## INVISIBLE POWER

As soon as I got to the office one early morning, one of my staff members called my attention to something they discovered that morning which must have happened overnight because it wasn't so at the close of work the previous day. He led me to our hall facility and showed me some burnt cables and about 70 percent of our electric bulbs and other appliances all burnt and all these happened because something went wrong in the circuit box.

As I looked at the scenario, it got me thinking about how this whole fire was caused by travelling current and yet we could not see the current but we could see the effects of it – The burnt cables, the black smoke effects on the walls, the dead bulbs, fans, television sets and so on. However, under the right conditions, it can give light, it can power air-conditioners, it can make fan blades rotate, run heavy machines and a lot of other things. It dawned on me that this is exactly how the healing current of God works.

We cannot see this power, but when it is applied, blind eyes will open, deaf ears will hear, dumb tongues will be loosed, the lame will walk the dying and even the dead would resurrect, life will flow and on the converse, can also afflict and destroy. We may not see the cause but we can always see the effects because the cause is spiritual and the effect is natural.

Romans 1:20 *"For the invisible things of him from the creation of the world are clearly seen, being understood by the things that are made, even his eternal power and God head: so that they are without excuse."* KJV

*"Gods eternal power and character cannot be seen but from the beginning of creation, God has shown what these are like by all he has made. That's why those people don't have any excuse"* CEV.

*"There are things about God that people cannot see - His eternal power and all that makes him God. But since the beginning of the world, those things have been easy for people to understand. They are made clear in what God has made. So people have no excuse for the evil they do"* ERV.

One day, I said to the Lord in prayer, 'Lord, if this power is not real, I don't want it, and if it's real, I want to see it manifest when there is no choir, no lights, no hypes. After all, Apostle Peter categorically told the lame man at the beautiful gate that he had something invisible but tangible and undeniable to offer him when he said,

*"...I don't have any silver or gold for you. But I'll give you what I have. In the name of Jesus Christ the Nazarene, get up and walk!"* Acts.3:6 (NLT).

I remember, in 2015, My friend, Rev. George Amadi flew in from the UK to purchase a car for his dad. As we were checking out one of the cars, when I saw a young man hopping on crutches and I was immediately drawn to him. God knows I hate to see people in pain.

It was in the open and passers-by stopped to watch as I prayed for him on the street of Alausa, Ikeja. In a split moment, I took the crutches from him and commanded him to walk. He was scared to the bone and I knew it. He said to me, "Sir, the doctors told me not to put it on the floor because the fibula is broken" Well, I encouraged him to put his weight on it. He did, and to the amazement of all he started walking with no pain. I was broken by the sight of that suffering baby.

He immediately invited me into his house to pray for his son who was in agony and had been throwing up all day.

He too got healed, the vomiting stopped at one command and strength came back to his body and you could see it.

His entire family, Including his mother, received Christ into their hearts right there. Just a few hours later, while we were in church, a text message came in from the wife sharing excitedly of how the husband is running all around the house.

Church, lets come out of our closet and go help people. This power works, if we work it. The world needs it.

Let us do it! It is for all believers, not for an exclusive few.

You can do it too, if you will come out to help people with no strings attached.

The kingdom of God is here! And the divine current will flow in real time from and through those who believe.

*"Whoever believes on me, as the scripture has said, out of his belly shall flow CURRENTS of living waters"* John 7:38.

Indeed, time is a veil and as long as we are stuck on this side of life wrapped up in time, we cannot see what's on the other side of life — The spiritual side. The realities of the spirit realm are even more authentic than the things we see with our optical eyes.

The other day, fifty armed men wanted to arrest a prophet and his servant. The servant was so scared by the sight of the fifty soldiers he saw until the prophet prayed for God to open his eyes. God did, and he saw thousands of armed and dangerous supernatural allies standing with them and ready to fight for them. Immediately, all his fears disapeared.

**66**
**One vision into the supernatural realm can dismantle a life time of fear. This life is bigger than your optical eyes can see.** **99**

There are a whole lot of activities going on around you right now that you are not even aware of.

I went to minister in a friend's church – Prophetic Assembly in Sabongida, Ora, Edo State and at the end of the meeting, I made an altar call for salvation. Among those that came forward was a young man on crutches. On seeing him, I called him out and asked him what happened to his legs. He told me he had a terrible accident at his place of work. He worked at a factory with heavy duty machines and in one of his routines, something went wrong. There was a malfunction and the machine fell on one of his legs and scattered the bones. They had to gather the pieces and framed them together with wood (a local way of bracing broken bones in Africa) just so it can look like a complete leg. He had several operations without any solution and couldn't walk for years. However, in less than two minutes I laid hands on him and commanded bones to find their bones just like the case of Ezekiel's valley.

To the amazement of all, the bones joined and he threw away his crutches and began to walk unaided.

Two days later, he was back on the field, playing football (soccer). Anything that can make that happen must be real. We can't see the power, but we know something flowed into him by the results we see.

Rom 1:11 *says, "For I long to see you, so that I might share with you some spiritual gift that can make you stronger. "*CTB Translation.

One day, my daughter, Juanita came over to my bedroom and asked to speak with me. I noticed the look on her face. She didn't look too happy and I thought someone upset her but that wasn't the case. She actually came to tell me she had found out the reason why one of her shoes was always tighter than the other. Initially, I didn't realize where she was going with it and I said, "Oh sorry about that, I never knew you were going through that," but then I realized she wanted something more. I had to ask her, "anything else?"

And she said softly, "Dad, can you pray about something like this?" Then it dawned on me, she was expecting a miracle so I assured her she could get it right away if she really wanted one. I felt the switch come on.'

Her left foot was bigger than the right one but she wanted the smaller one to become equal with the left foot. I asked her to sit on my bed with her legs stretched out and the toes looking up. The difference was so obvious. How come we didn't notice that before then? She was nine at that time. I commanded the right foot to grow and become equal with the left one, and then a dramatic miracle ensued before our very eyes. It grew out and became equal with the other. My God! You needed to be there to see the look on her face when she screamed, "Daddy! How did you do that? It was priceless. And I replied, "that's what I've been telling you about - The reality of the supernatural power of God. Glory to God!

*It was by faith that Moses left the land of Egypt, not fearing the king's anger. He kept right on going because he kept his eyes on the one who is invisible.* Heb.11:27

Moses made vital decisions based on invisible visions. The spiritual realm is invisible to the natural eyes, it cannot be perceived by natural senses but is real and really affect and influence nature and the natural realm.

# CHAPTER 4

# CONDUCTORS

1. In electrical engineering, a **conductor** is an object or type of material that allows the flow of an electrical current in one or more directions. A metal wire is a common electrical conductor.

An **electrical conductor** is a substance in which **electrical** charge carriers, usually electrons, move easily from atom to atom with the application of voltage.

2. A conductor is a PERSON who directs the PERFORMANCE of an orchestra or choir.

3. A conductor is also a PERSON IN CHARGE of a train, a street car or a public conveyance.

Following the key words here, we can correctly extrapolate that conductors are people in charge of certain performances.

Just as electrical conductors allow current to flow and be discharged to different directions, believers function like conductors. As a matter of fact, they are human conductors of God's power on earth.

Do you know that the **human body is a good** conductor **of electricity**? That means that electricity flows easily through our bodies. Why? Because electricity moves quickly through water - and the human body is 70 percent water! I believe that this is the reason why the human body is still one of the best conductors of the anointing of God.

It is amazing how God would commit such powers into the hands of men. What this means is that to a great extent, men are responsible for the magnitude of God's power we experience on earth.

The fact that the power is flowing from me towards you does not mean it would flow into you and the fact that the power resides in me, doesn't mean it would ever help anybody including me.

*"Unto him who is able to do exceeding abundantly above all that we ask or think, ACCORDING TO THE POWER THAT WORKETH IN US."* Eph.3:20.

**66 Potential energy is good, but kinetic energy is better. It is not the resident power that matters but the active power. 99**

It's interesting to hear believers quote this scripture with particular reference to how great and mighty our God is without examining the capitalised words in the above text. God does not lack power to do anything he wishes to do, he can do anything but we must understand that the extent to which God's power works for us is according to the power that works in us.

When you confessed Christ as your saviour, you received power. But for many, that power has been lying dormant. That **POWER IS YOUR FAITH.**

The question is, is your faith working or is it dead? Remember, faith without works is dead. (James 2:20). For you to experience the mightiness and greatness of God, his power needs to start working in you. What is the current state of that power you received when you got born again.

When you received Jesus into your heart, you received **DIVINITY** on your inside. God now resides in you. For you to see God at work in you, you need to activate the power within by speaking with him in the spirit. God wants to have fellowship with you so you can receive a rub off of His mind.

It would take only the right mindset to be able to conduct the power of GOD. To be a conductor of divine energy, you have to also believe that God can use you even with all your human limitations.

## THE HEALING CURRENT

"A. A. Allen, my favourite healing evangelist, was clearly one of the most important revivalists to emerge in the early days of the healing revival and was one who ploughed on with grass-roots healing revivalism for over twenty years until his death in 1970. Charismatic and controversial, this comparative latecomer to the revival was known as 'the boldest of the bold' amongst his peers and loved by thousands of his followers.

Many notable miracles are on record, but one of the most significant occurred March, 1959 in the ministry of A. A. Allen. It was the account of a four year old boy who received 26 creative miracles in one service.

R. W. Schambach was A. A. Allen's worship leader at the time and also shares his eye-witness account of this miracle and his role in it.

He relates how the mother of this young boy came to him on the last day of a week of healing meetings. This faithful mother had traveled from her home in Knoxville, TN to Birmingham because of her desire for the young boy to be supernaturally healed. That was his only hope since the best of the medical field had given up on him and gave no hope for survival.

The young four year old lad was born with 26 major diseases. He was blind, deaf, and dumb and his tongue protruded from his mouth and rested upon his chin. His arms and legs were deformed and twisted against his body and totally useless. He had no feet and remained curled in a fetal position from the day he was born. He had no male organs and every other major organ in his body suffered from numerous complications. Most doctors said that he would not live to his first birthday. Nevertheless, he was now four years old and in desperate need of God's touch.

The young mother had been to every service for a week and the final day had come. In those days the ministers used prayer cards to determine who would be prayed for. Unfortunately, her prayer card was never called. She personally went to brother Schambach and asked if he would help get her son to the man of God for prayer. Brother Schambach promised that he would, but that never became necessary since the Lord had other plans.

When the service began, A. A. Allen took an offering that challenged the people into the supernatural realm of faith. As a gesture of faith, this young mother was the first to put $20 in the offering. Like the widow woman in the Lord's ministry, it was all that she had. As the man of God began the service, he stopped his preaching and announced that he was going into a spiritual vision.

In his vision, Allen found himself in the maternity ward of a hospital where a small boy was just born. He saw the doctors pronounce a death sentence on the lad with 26 major illnesses.

He then watched in his vision as the mother entered an old Ford automobile and drove to that very meeting in Birmingham, AL. He then called for the mother to bring the young boy for prayer.

## THE POWER OF GOD OVERSHADOWS THE YOUNG BOY

When he offered the prayer of faith, R. W. Schambach testified that he saw with his own eyes, the power of God overshadow the boy.

1. First, the tongue of the little fellow corrected itself into his mouth.

2. Next, pools of light entered his eye sockets and beautiful brown eyes were supernaturally created.

3. He then watched his bones begin to snap and crack as his legs and arms came into their perfect place.

4. Then, Schambach watched as the two legs that had no feet suddenly began to change as feet were supernaturally created for the young boy right before the 3,000 in attendance.

5. All of his internal organs were perfectly restored.

6. Finally, the tongue of the young lad was supernaturally allowed to speak his first words...Mamma.

This is a token of the kind of creative miracles we are promised in this generation" - Bob Jones & Paul Keith Davis.

Acts 10:38 *How God anointed Jesus of Nazareth with the Holy Ghost and with power: who went about doing good, and healing all that were oppressed of the devil; for God was with him.*

I have heard this scripture explained a couple of times, but I've never heard this first part, talked about by anybody – the part that says, "How God anointed Jesus of Nazareth…" As the Lord was dealing with me on this subject, He emphasized the first word in the text, "HOW" And he said to me, HOW is very important here.

We know he anointed Jesus, we have seen the results of the anointing but we need to know how he anointed Jesus. He said to me, "Son, if you understand how Jesus got anointed, you will know how you can also get anointed"

There is power in knowledge but understanding is one step above knowledge. We need a proper understanding of how the power of God works

We live in a day and time when we cannot do without the power of God. These are the days prophesied by Prophet Isaiah, "Arise, shine; for thy light is come, and the glory of the Lord is risen upon thee.

*For, behold, the darkness shall cover the earth and gross darkness the people: but the Lord shall rise upon thee and his glory shall be seen upon thee"* Isaiah 60:1-2

These are the end times when gross darkness is covering the people of the world but for the children of God, the glory of God would be seen on them and he described that glory as LIGHT.

Doesn't that sound familiar? Light is one of the results, effects, or manifestations of electric current. The same way the healing current or the glory of God in us produces light through us. Light in this context, represents the good works we produce as a result of the current flowing in us.

What exactly are good works? I'm glad you asked. "Let your light so shine before men, that they may see your good works, and glorify your father which is in heaven" (1)Good works can be seen by men (2) Good works glorify God. Here it

*"How God anointed Jesus of Nazareth with the Holy Ghost and with power: who went about DOING GOOD (Works) and healing all that were oppressed of the devil; for God was with him".*

Our Lord was anointed with divine current so that he went about doing good works that were described as healing the sick, casting out devils, raising the dead and literally, destroying all the works of the devil. This is the summary of the life of Jesus as described in the four gospels.

*"For this purpose the son of God was manifested, that he might destroy the works of the devil."* I John 3:8.

*"The thief cometh not but for to steal, and to kill and to destroy: I am come that they might have life and that they might have it more abundantly."* John 10:10.

We have been called to let our lights shine. Light does not shine unless it is connected to a power source. We heal the sick, cast out devils do all kinds of good works because the power of God is working in us to produce results.

**Light does not shout, it shines.**

We have not been anointed just to talk about his power but to show forth his power by producing light for the world to see and for God to be glorified in the earth. If we must truly shine forth we must get connected to the divine current which is what produces the good works.

# CHAPTER 5

# POWER GENERATORS

*And these signs will follow those who believe; in My name they will cast out demons; they will speak with new tongues.* - Mark 16:17.

Jesus of Nazareth was a generator of power, and if we must do the works he did, we must identify the secret of his powerful and colorful ministry. How did he pray?

He was always praying in tongues. You say Man of God, can you prove that? Of course, I can and I will.

The Apostles came to Jesus one day and and pleaded with him to teach them how to pray. They observed how he would always withdraw to the deserts and mountains to pray for hours, especially in the wee hours of the day.

They heard him pray in a way they had never known. They also observed the effects of his prayers on the sick, demon possessed and the sinner. They didn't need a prophet to tell them that his kind of prayers were more effective than those of the Pharisees and the temple Rabbis, hence, they voiced out,

"Rabbi, teach us how to pray."

How can you pray like that? What words are you saying, what are you asking for? The only way you can pray all night till dawn is when you are praying with a supernatural language and ability.

One day he got before a dead girl. He opened His mouth and said *"Talitha Cumi"* interpreted to mean, little girl arise! (Mark 5:41). It wasn't translated. It was interpreted. There is a difference between translation and interpretation. You can translate a human and natural language but you interpret tongues.

The other day, while he was on the cross he spoke a language that confused everybody who listened and heard him. They didn't know what he said. He didn't speak Greek, Hebrew or Aramaic. He spoke a language that none of them could understand when he said *"Eloi, Eloi, lama sabachthani"*. Mark 15:34).

They all began to guess what he was trying to say. Some even said he was calling on Elijah to save him. Some said he was calling for deliverance but what he said was interpreted again to us by the gift of interpretation of tongues. And it means,

Jesus was the only man on earth who had the holy ghost in him which accounts for why he was the only one at that time who could speak the language of the spirit. (Colossians 2:9). We cannot speak in that language until the Holy Spirit comes to dwell in us.

When the disciples asked Jesus to teach them to pray like he prayed he didn't teach them how to pray in tongues because it's not a language to be learnt, but a gift to be received.

He taught them to pray a prayer that would prepare them to receive the Promise of the Father which is the Holy Spirit. At that time, Jesus had not died and his blood had not been shed so He taught them to pray for the advent of God's kingdom. Matthew 6:9-13.

The Holy Ghost is the one who brings the kingdom of God to men.

The bible lets us know that righteousness, peace and joy in the Holy Ghost that is the kingdom of God. Romans 14:17. When we talk about the kingdom of God, we are talking about all that the Holy Spirit brought into the world - The righteousness of God, the peace of God and the Joy of the Lord.

When the Holy Ghost comes into your life, the righteousness of God has come in, the peace of God has come in and the Joy of the Lord has come in. In the presence of God, there is fullness of Joy and at his right hand there are pleasures forevermore.

Whenever the Holy Ghost comes into a life, God's presence has come in. This is what we mean when we say God lives in us and when we say Jesus lives in us. We are referring to the Holy Spirit and not Jesus as a man because the man, Christ Jesus is currently seated at the right hand of the Father in glory. It's the Holy Ghost who is God Himself that brings the presence of the Father to us. As sons and daughters of God, washed by the blood of Jesus, He lives in us today. He the Spirit brings the power that works in us. Ephesians 3:20.

It is now our responsibility to generate the power of God by the Holy Ghost who lives in us and as a result, when we pray with the spirit, that's not our prayer. That is the Spirit of God praying for us which generates the power that produces activities like the working of miracles, casting out devils and healing the sick.

The spirit in our Lord Jesus, moved him to the wilderness where he would pray, fast and be tempted by Satan for a period of forty days and forty nights. Why? So He can go there and generate the power needed to successfully accomplish his ministry, destiny and assignment in the world. Resultantly, at the end of his 40 days fasting, praying and spiritual warfare, the bible lets us know that he came out in the power of the Spirit. Luke 4:14.

Sweetheart, this is how God anointed Jesus of Nazareth - in the place of prayer. What kind of prayer? The prayer of tongues!

If he was moved by the Spirit into the wilderness to pray, and according to the Word of God, He returned in the power of the Spirit, it only makes sense, that when He prayed in the wilderness, He must have prayed in the Spirit.

If you dont pray in the spirit, you cannot come out in the power of the Spirit. This is how Jesus was anointed. When Jesus left the wilderness in the power of the spirit, the next place he went to, was the Synagogue where he eventually healed a man with a withered hand by the power of the Spirit and guess what?

Just before He performed the miracle, He announced to the people what had happened to him. Guess what his announcement was?

*"The spirit of the Lord God is upon me because He hath anointed me to preach the gospel to the poor; He hath sent me to heal the broken hearted, to preach deliverance to the captives, and recovering of sight to the blind, to set at liberty them that are bruised, to preach the acceptable year of the Lord."* Luke 4:18,19.

When did that anointing happen? It happened while he was praying with the Spirit in the wilderness, for forty days and forty nights. Glory to God!

# PRAYING IN THE SPIRIT

A logging foreman sold a farmer a chainsaw. He said, "This is guaranteed to chop down 50 trees a day." The farmer was impressed with that. A week later, the farmer stormed back through the front door, threw the saw on the counter, and demanded his money back. "There's something wrong with this saw. There's no way it'll do 50 trees a day. It can hardly do three trees a day!" The foreman grabbed the saw, pulled the cord, and the saw went, "Bzzzzzzz." The farmer jumped back, eyes wide open: "Hey, what's that noise?" For so many Christians, God's power is available to them, but they simply don't know how to access it. Praying in the Spirit is the ancient secret of generating power in the kingdom of God.

Praying in the Spirit is the means by which our redeemed human spirit communicates directly with God's Spirit. Intended to be used for more than just communicating with God in prayer, it is also designed to be a power producer to enhance the operation of all the other gifts and graces of God.

For these reasons it could be considered one of the greatest gifts of the Holy Spirit that a Christian can receive.

Praying in the Holy Spirit is the ability given to believers that allows them to pray in a supernatural language that bypasses mental tollgates.

It is also sometimes referred to as praying in tongues or praying in unknown languages.

Your spirit is the purest part of you so when you pray in your spirit it is the purest kind of prayer, hence, the most powerful way to pray.

## Built-In Power Plants

*"But you, beloved, building yourselves up on your most holy faith, praying in the Holy Spirit."* (Jude 20)

A lot of people get into issues of life and expect to see a manifestation of God's power but never get to see it and at the end of the day are weighed down by their situations and then begin to blame God. They ask questions like "God why?" why? If you have power why don't you do it? Now this is what I want to straighten out. There is no controversy about the efficacy of God's power or that all power belongs to God.

He wasn't going to violate his own authority.

## 66 For God's gifts and his call can never be withdrawn. 99

God stands by what he does and stands by what he has declared or spoken.

Because God has given the earth to the sons of men to govern, he would need man to give him license to interfere in human affairs. This is the very reason why God sometimes doesn't get involved in what you do even when you think he should. Why? Because there is a certain principle that must be activated in order to involve God in your personal affairs. It is called prayer.

## 66 To pray is to give God permission to invade your space. 99

In order for you to see the power of God here on the earth, you must involve God through prayers. Authority on earth has been given to man. God no longer regulates it; man does by the temperature of his prayer life.

Does God want us to experience His power in the place of deliverance, healing, restoration? Yes! But does God always manifest his power because you need it? No! Does God always manifest his power because you want it? No! And I will tell you the reason why. God is a God of integrity, He is called the righteous God, and he is a God that says something and honors and respects what he says. When God says something he stands by it.

God said; I have exalted my Word above my name. Now this is very interesting; the word of God and the name of God are the two elements we are going to look into:

The word of God stands for the integrity of God, whereas the name of God stands for the personality of God and the personality has to do with the image that has been formed about him. In other words, when you hear his name what comes to your mind? Do you see a weak, tired, and impotent God?

Were there times when you expected God to show his strength but he never did and it made you think that God was weak? God says, because I have already put my word in place, every time a situation occurs where my name will have to clash with my words, I would rather honor my Word than rescue my Name. If it would take you to think I am weak just because I want to keep to my Word, I would rather keep my Word and leave you to have your own ideas of who I am. I would rather be seen as shamed and disgraced in your eyes than to break my own Word or principle.

For instance, when God made man, He gave man dominion and authority over the face of the earth and he says that man will become the God of the earth.

Then God said, *"Let us make mankind in our image, in our likeness, so that they may rule over the fish in the sea and the birds in the sky, over the livestock and all the wild animals, and over all the creatures that move along the ground."* Genesis 1:26.

*"The heavens belong to the LORD, but he has given the earth to all humanity."* Psalm 115:16

**" The temperature of your prayer life determines the amount of 'godness' you manifest. "**

*The bible says, "Now unto him that is able to do exceeding abundantly above all that we ask or think, according to the power that worketh in us"* Eph.3:20

There is no controversy about the ability of God. What we have to deal with is the clause at the end of the text that reads; "...according to the power that worketh in us." When the day of Pentecost was fully come, the Holy Spirit was sent from heaven as a gift to the Church of Christ and ever since, has not left the earth. When the Holy Spirit came, He came with the power of God.

It is in the nature of the flame to burn away the oil by which it is fed. ...It is all an outgoing of oil; and if there be no incoming thereof, the flame will not burn long. E.M. Goulburn

# POWER PACK

*"But you will receive power when the Holy Spirit comes upon you. And you will be my witnesses, telling people about me everywhere--in Jerusalem, throughout Judea, in Samaria, and to the ends of the earth." Acts1:18.*

Right now, the power of God is on earth and man has been delegated by God to rule and to govern the earth and this means that heaven no longer regulates the power, earth does. How does this happen? When a man gets born again in Christ, he receives the anointing of the Spirit which remains dormant until it is activated by the Person of the Holy Spirit.
When you purchase a new phone, it comes with ability to perform in a whole lot of ways, but not until it is activated by the service provider, you can't even make or receive a call, talk less of using other apps with it. This is how the power of God works. When we receive Christ, that new life we receive is heaven's power pack in our belly that can only be harnessed and enjoyed after activation.

The only limits that we know that God has, are the limits that we put on Him. Nick Vujicic

The power of God in your belly only works as long as you work it. I live in Nigeria; and in Nigeria, we have power supplied to the nation from the dams,

Nigeria has about 264 dams and one of them is called Khanji dam. It is the major dam that supplies power to the nation.

The dam is a generator of power. But then, because it doesn't supply enough power to the whole nation, individual citizens have to look for ways to generate power for themselves. As a result, we use a lot of generators in our nation. For instance, in one of our churches, we have a 100KVA generator that powers our services. Since we started out in 2003, we have never used electricity coming from Khanji dam on any given Sunday. We have always had our own power supply generators. Every child of God ought to be a power generator to supply power within their own sphere of influence. We are called to supply light to a world full of darkness.

"...Bishop Bill Hamon of Christian International Ministries gave a fantastic analogy of an electrical power plant utilizing a river and reservoir of water to produce electricity.

When a dam is built on a river, it causes the water to back up and form a reservoir. The reservoir water is the same water that will eventually flow through a turbine and continue on as a river.

However, in the process of producing power, the water must become more active, noisy, and turbulent as it goes through the turbines.

Spiritually speaking, each believer has their own built-in power plant, which can produce the supernatural power of God in and through their lives. The water could be compared to being filled with the Holy Spirit. When upstream from the dam, it does not produce supernatural power until it flows through the gate (mouth) and turns the turbine (the unity of God's Spirit and our spirit) to produce power.

When we pray in the Spirit, it is like the river starts flowing and activating our spiritual turbine. The activation of the turbine is what starts the chain reaction that produces power that enables things to work.

The Word says in John 7:37-39 English Standard Version (ESV)

*"37 On the last day of the feast, the great day, Jesus stood up and cried out, "If anyone thirsts, let him come to me and drink. 38 Whoever believes in me, as[a] the Scripture has said, 'Out of his heart will flow rivers of living water.'" 39 Now this he said about the Spirit, whom those who believed in him were to receive, for as yet the Spirit had not been given, because Jesus was not yet glorified."*

# Acts 6:4 Context

1. And in those days, when the number of the disciples was multiplied, there arose a murmuring of the Grecians against the Hebrews, because their widows were neglected in the daily ministration.

2. Then the twelve called the multitude of the disciples unto them, and said, It is not reason that we should leave the word of God, and serve tables.

3. Wherefore, brethren, look ye out among you seven men of honest report, full of the Holy Ghost and wisdom, whom we may appoint over this business.

4. But we will give ourselves continually to prayer, and to the ministry of the word.

The Early Christians understood that they could not neglect prayer. They were a praying church and how great and mighty things they achieved in prayer. Even when they became very busy in ministry, they did not allow business to get in the way of prayer. In the literal text it says,

"We will persevere and give ourselves to the prayer..."

Pay attention to the words 'the prayer' not just a prayer. It was a definite article meaning a determiner that introduces a noun phrase and implies that the thing mentioned has already been mentioned and was common knowledge.

The Early church comprehended that 'praying in tongues' was the prayer. Praying in tongues was known as the prayer. There are many kinds of prayers in the Scripture but Tongues is the ultimate prayer in the New Testament. The Early Church gave much time and attention to it. This was common knowledge to the early disciples and it should be so in the modern church.

Prayer, especially praying in tongues, is a vital aspect to our spiritual growth, walking in the supernatural and being sensitive in the spirit. There is no way around it! If you want to grow in the anointing, it is imperative that you become a person of prayer. Jesus was a man of prayer as was the Apostle Paul and the early church was birthed and based on prayer. The Holy Writ shows that prayer and specially 'tongues' played a very prominent role in the life of the early church and it must play a prominent role in your life.

If you want to grow in the anointing, it is imperative that you become a person of prayer.

One of the greatest ministers who ever graced this earth was Reverend John G. Lake. Although he went through terrible hardships, he was a world shaker. What was the secret to John G. Lake's deep revelations, extraordinary manifestations, and the success of his ministry?

Here is an excerpt from his own mouth:

"I want to talk with the utmost frankness and say to you, that tongues have been the making of my ministry. It is that peculiar communication with God when God reveals to my soul the truth I utter to you day by day in the ministry.

Many times, I climb out of bed, take my pencil and pad, and jot down the beautiful things of God, the wonderful things of God that He talks out in my spirit and reveals to my heart." Notice these words: "Tongues have been the making of my ministry."

Tongues will be the making of your life.

Another great man who knew the power of praying in tongues was Smith Wigglesworth. Here was an uneducated plumber who, when he partook of the blessing of tongues, was transformed into the apostle of faith. The miracles, boldness, and manifestation of the supernatural became evident in his life and ministry.

The church and the world are waiting for endtime apostles who will be carriers of power and deliverance. You can be so as you develop the habit of praying in tongues! Apart from the obvious and common knowledge ones, let me list two benefits that you will enjoy as you partake of this marvelous blessing:-

1. Praying in tongues is strengthening your inner self with might.

Ephesians 3:16 tells us, "That He would grant you, according to the riches of His glory, to be strengthened with might by His Spirit in the inner man."

The Weymouth New Testament words it like this, "To grant you—in accordance with the wealth of His glorious perfections—to be strengthened by His Spirit with power penetrating to your inmost being." To strengthen means "to make stronger." It also means "to increase in strength and force."

According to the apostle Paul, when you pray in tongues, you are strengthening or fortifying your spirit man with might. Obviously, he would know more about the might of tongues, as he declared to the Corinthian saints that he prayed in tongues more than them all (see 1 Cor. 14:18).

The word 'might' is the Greek word 'dunamis', and it means "miracle power and explosive power." The more you pray in the spirit, the more you are increasing in spiritual force on the inside of you. The more you pray in tongues, the more explosive power and miraculous power are growing inside of you.

How can you be depressed when the strength of God is within you? Just like barbells will build up your arms, praying in tongues will build up your spirit. When your spirit is strong, it will help to keep that flesh body of yours in line. The more you pray in the spirit, the more you are increasing in spiritual force within.

2. Praying in tongues is part of the offensive of the armor of God. It is the lance that will shoot down the enemy.

Ephesians 6:13-18;"*Wherefore take unto you the whole armour of God, that ye may be able to withstand in the evil day, and having done all, to stand. Stand therefore, having your loins girt about with truth, and having on the breastplate of righteousness; And your feet shod with the preparation of the gospel of peace; Above all, taking the shield of faith, wherewith ye shall be able to quench all the fiery darts of the wicked. And take the helmet of salvation, and the sword of the Spirit, which is the word of God: Praying always with all prayer and supplication in the Spirit, and watching thereunto with all perseverance and supplication for all saints.*"

"The whole armor of God": Pay attention to the words 'whole armor' referring to the Greek word panoplia, meaning "whole, complete set." It was a word used to depict the full armor of a hoplite or heavily-armed Roman soldier. Whenever the Roman soldier would put on his full armor, there were seven things that he would put on. The apostle Paul listed all the other Roman weaponries by name except for the lance.

No Roman panoply would be complete without the lance. Since six is "the number of man" and seven is "the number of God," seven stands for completion. That is why in the Old Testament we see and read of the seven feasts of Israel, seven sacrifices, seven furnitures of the tabernacle, seven lamps of the candlestick, seven pillars of wisdom, and seven cities of refuge to name a few. The New Testament, specifically the Book of Revelation talks of the seven churches, Seven Spirits of God, seven golden candlesticks, seven stars, seven lamps of fire, seven seals, seven horns and seven trumpets to name a few.

God does things in sevens, and the seventh weaponry of the armor of God is the lance of prayer in the spirit. The Roman lance was called a pilum. It was the typical legionary weapon together with the short sword gladius.

It was designed to penetrate the shield as well as the soldier holding it, and to bend upon impact to make it unusable for another opponent. The pilum was used for long distances by throwing it, and for shorter distances they would use it to charge. It was a very offensive weapon. Praying in tongues is an aggressive and offensive weapon to put holes in the cover of the devil. The lance of tongues is designed to paralyze the movements of the devil against your life. No wonder the devil fights tongues so much, as it causes great harm in his kingdom.

When Peter's life was threatened by Herod, the church tapped into 'the unceasing prayer of tongues' and reversed the death sentence and demonic assignment. Tongues will make your progress unstoppable! Pray in tongues!" - Sid Roth.

I believe strongly that we are the generation that will enter into this glory. We are the generation that will manifest the power of God like no other before us.

Thank God for testimonies and stories we have heard about men of old, we have even read stories about God's generals like William Branham, Alexander Dowie, A.A Allen, John Graham Lakes and a host of others.

We have heard of amazing exploits God wrought through these men of God in the past. However, all these are nothing to be compared with what we are about to see and which we are already seeing in our generation. We are seeing the power of God like never before.

For those who will take time out to fellowship with God in the Spirit, you will tap into a well of power and cause it to flow out as rivers to this generation.

It's time to break the old wells and turn them into rivers of liquid life. It's time for this generation to wake up and tap into this divine power that can heal the sick and raise the dead, twist nature, make a nonsense of natural elements and principles, make amputated legs grow out and bring back missing body organs.

We have seen mind blowing miracles in our ministry where the blind receive their sight without eye sockets and the barren conceive and bare children without womb but we are trusting God to see more.

Like Paul, *"that I may know him in the power of his resurrection and fellowship of his suffering"*.

I have seen God do things. I have seen God manifest his power and his glory in unprecedented forms. But I'm not satisfied. I am hungry for more. I am looking forward to days of heaven on earth where I would heal the sick en masse, not with my hands, neither with words but with my thoughts.

## CHAPTER 6

# PHOTOGRAPHIC TECHNOLOGY

"Imagination is more powerful than information" - Albert Einstein.

Information is limited to what is known but imagination is infinite.
You are not permitted to come accross a blessing that has never crossed your mind. If by any chance you come across one, know that its only just crossing your way to the true owner. Such is called an **ACCIDENTAL BLESSING**. It won't be long before it becomes obvious to all that it was truly an accident because you won't be able to keep it for long. You cannot own a realm you have not imagined.

The moment you become a conductor, it is your responsibility to direct, control and channel the power to the appropriate ends. It is the same electric current supplied to a house that powers the bulbs, the pressing iron, the refrigerator, deep freezer, television and all other electrical appliances in the house so multitask. The same power that casts out devils, heals the sick, raises the dead and can also readjust nature and break the laws of time. The extent of results we see depends on our voltage capacity and the skilfulness of our imaginative abilities. Imagination directs the power to new terrains and tells it what to do.

Imagination is a powerful gift given to the body of Christ that is seldom used. God has so much in stock for us but the EYES of our understanding must be opened to see and receive Eph 1:18

Your mind is a camera. Photographic Cameras are prototypes of your mind. There's however, no camera with a pixel as sharp as your mind.
Everything is a product of imagination, if the mind can capture it, then you expect to see manifestations. The blessing of God that comes to you is commensurate with your mindset.
In fact, **GOD CANNOT HELP YOU BEYOND YOUR MINDSET.**

In Isaiah 14:13, Lucifer , the devil was arrested and cast down just because he imagined himself as God. He simply said in his heart that he would ascend the heavens... And God found him guilty for that because God understand that imagination is the path to eventual manifestation. That's how powerful the realm of imagination is. In the spirit realm, thoughts are concrete.

In Genesis 11:6, while the people gathered to build the Tower of Babel, God came down to see and said "...Now nothing they purpose or imagine to do will be withheld from them. Imagination always directs the flow of God's power.

Again, in Matt. 5:28, Jesus said whosoever looks at a woman to lust after her HAS ALREADY committed adultery in his heart. This means that imagining it is as good as doing it. If according to Jesus, to imagine it is to commit it, then we can conclude that imagining it is as good as having it, imagining it is as good as building it, imagining it is as good as driving it, imagining it is as good as becoming it. We can go on and on and on.

The questions are: Have u been imagining at all? If yes, what have u been imagining? Do you know you can snap the picture in your mind and see that breakthrough come to pass? Do you know that with your imagination you can communicate your desires?

The woman with the issue of blood directed the flow of healing current towards her situation when she said to herself (Imagination) "If I can only touch the hem of his garment, I shall be made whole".

The church must take back the gift of imagination. Several blessings have been locked up and shut down simply because we have not learnt to use the power of imagination. God wants to arrest you at the point of your imagination. Dare to dream big, think big and see yourself become big.

This same power that heals the sick and casts out devils can also turn a pauper into a billionaire. The only reason it hasn't happened to you yet is because it has not even crossed your mind. Capturing the image in your mind, is a giant step in the right direction.

# Testimonies
### With Photographs

She could not stand up straight due to chronic waist pain. After prayer, all the pains left and she was able to stand, run and jump all over the place unaided

**Glory to God!**

This woman went totally blind as a teenager after an accident. After prayers, the Lord restored her sight and she was able to describe in details what I was wearing and holding and mimicked every movement I made. He is still busy today!

**Glory to God!**

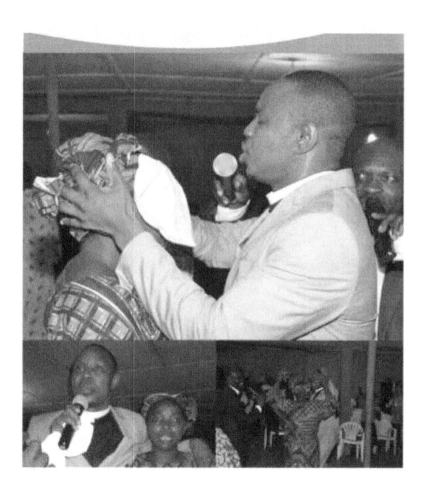

On Monday, May 5, 2013, this lady received prayers for
Supernatural Weight Loss and lost weight immediately
and the suit jacket she wore became oversize.
Right now, she is putting on a dress she hadn't been able
to wear in two years in this photograph.

**To God be the glory!**

This brother suffered gunshot injuries. he was shot four times in four different places. He came with a walker; but he was completely healed tonight, running all over church unaided. God still works miracles.

Praise God!

Getting ready to check out of the hotel on Friday after a two day conference in Benin City, Nigeria, with Pastor Joshua Ogu, I was introduced to a pretty young lady who was brought by two brothers so I could pray for her. I was told she became stone deaf and dumb at the age of three. Immediately after prayers, she started hearing from both ears and spoke words after me for the first time since age three. Her reaction was priceless. Things like this make me want to preach much more!
I love Jesus; I love this gospel
of the Kingdom.
**Glory!**

**Another stiff arm
healed by the power of
God's healing current**

She lost her sight and hearing due to
ageing. After prayer, both sight and
hearing were restored and she was able
to identify the colour of my suit. She was
so shocked she asked me if I was sure it
won't return as she had suffered so much
as a result of this predicament.

**Glory to God!**
More Lord, More!

I called her out by word of knowledge. She could barely raise her arm; but after prayers, see what God Did!
There is healing in Jesus' name. Glory!

This man could
not walk without the aid of a walker due to partial
paralysis in the left leg, after prayer, his legs were able
to carry his weight without aid. I took the aid from him
and he walked around the auditorium freely.

Gory!
It's time to be free!!

Her stiff arm was
supernaturally healed by
the healing current of
God.

Deaf ears opened in Memphis, Tn.!
This man was stone deaf but the power of
God showed up and restored his hearing
and he broke down in tears on realizing
what the Lord just did for him.

**Glory to the
Most High God!**

She had an accident that left her on crutches for over a year due to broken bones that would not heal. During prayers in one of our Night of Correction services, the power of God came upon her and she lifted her crutches and began to walk with unassisted - something she hadn't been able to do in almost two years.

With International Worship
Leader, Don Moen 2015

With Evangelist And Gospel
Musician, Steve Brock 2012

With
International Healing Evangelist,
Pastor Benny Hinn 2017

## CHAPTER 7

## INSULATORS

An **electrical insulator** is a material whose internal **electric** charges do not flow freely, and therefore make it nearly impossible to conduct an **electric** current under the influence of an **electric** field. This contrasts with other materials, semiconductors and conductors, which conduct **electric** current more easily. The property that distinguishes an insulator is its resistivity; insulators have higher resistivity than semiconductors or conductors.

Some common insulator materials are **glass**, **plastic**, **rubber**, air, and **wood**.


2 Chronicles 20:20(KJV) - And they rose early in the morning, and went forth into the wilderness of Tekoa: and as they went forth, Jehoshaphat stood and said, Hear me, O Judah, and ye inhabitants of Jerusalem; Believe in the LORD your God, so shall ye be established; believe his prophets, so shall ye prosper.

Simply put, insulators cannot experience the anointing of God because they resist the flow of divine currents. You can never attract the anointing you do not respect. Some people are insulators of the anointing. It doesn't matter how anointed you are or what you do, you can never help them.

I know it's a struggle to honor those whom God has anointed. Do you want to know why? Because we judge people according to the flesh. We size them up with our eyes and determine whether or not they deserve our respect based on carnal standards.

2 Corinthians 5:16 is so clear. Do not evaluate people from a human point of view. You will get it all wrong. Judge by The Spirit.

Hence, if you are going to benefit from the anointing you have to respect the anointing. You don't have to get caught up in the person ministering. Put your focus on God. It's not about the person anyway. It's about the anointing that's on the person as a result of the presence of the Holy Spirit. God will deliver by the power of His Holy Spirit. Unbelief destroyed the power of the anointing in the lives of the people to whom Jesus ministered in Mark 6:1-6. The Bible is clear. He could not do any miracles among them except healing a few sick people because of their unbelief.

It didn't say He would not. It says, He could not. They were too familiar. They were too disrespectful. They cut off the miracle working power of God in the flesh. They were insulators. So, if that happened to Jesus where does that leave the rest of us?

"And he said unto his men, The LORD forbid that I should do this thing unto my master, the LORD'S anointed, to stretch forth mine hand against him, seeing he is anointed of the LORD" (1 Samuel 24:6).

David was a man who understood the anointing and had respect for the Lord's anointed. The Bible tells us how one day, Saul, with a band of three thousand chosen men sought for David, to kill him, but it was David who eventually had the opportunity to have Saul killed yet he refrained.

Though David went only as far as cutting off Saul's skirt while the latter slept, the Bible says,

"It came to pass afterward, that David's heart smote him, because he has cut off Saul's skirt. And he said unto his men, The Lord forbid that I should do this thing unto my master, the Lord's anointed, to stretch forth mine hand against him, seeing he is the anointed of the Lord. So David stayed his servants with these works, and suffered them not to rise against Saul..." (1 Samuel 24:5-7).

David recognized the anointing of God upon the life of Saul and had respect unto it.

Similarly, David's unequivocal respect for the anointing was further demonstrated when he ordered the death of the Amalekite who confessed to have killed Saul. He said to the man:

*"...Thy blood be upon thy head; for thy mouth hath testified against thee, saying, I have slain the LORD's anointed"* (2 Samuel 1:16).

David thus proved himself worthy of the anointing. God later testified of Him saying,

*"I have found David my servant; with my holy oil have I anointed him:* (Psalms 89:20).

Understand that what you respect, you attract. If you want to walk in the anointing of God's Spirit, you must have respect for the anointing, honour and respect God's anointed servants.

It is true that electricity has helped to remove darkness and increase human activity. Powerful lights are used in factories, schools, hospitals and in all other dark places where men have to work for the benefit of others or for themselves. Men are able to go anywhere even in the darkest of nights.

Electricity has also enabled men to increase the production of their goods. Huge machines are operated in large factories with the help of electricity for the manufacture of useful goods.

These machines work ceaselessly and produce enormous quantities of goods, which are distributed throughout the world, for the comfort of people in all parts of the earth. . Even to transport goods and people to the remotest regions of the earth, electricity is extremely useful. Land, air and sea transport are all assisted by the use of electricity. People can now travel in great comfort and ease for business or pleasure to any part of the world. In the same way, goods can be sent to all the corners of the earth with the greatest of ease.

Electricity is even used for the treatment of some people who suffer from peculiar diseases. In short, the use of electricity has changed the lives of men to such an extent that life without it is almost unthinkable.

However, as good as electricity is, it can be very dangerous if not controlled or properly handled by a professional.

Dangers of Electricity include a variety of hazards that include Electric Shock, Psychological Damage, Physical Burns, Neurological Damage and Ventricular fibrillation resulting in death.

Any form of energy, when not properly controlled or harnessed, can result in serious danger to those who use it.

Electricity at any voltage can be dangerous and should always be approached with caution. An electric shock can occur upon contact of a human or animal body with any source of voltage high enough to cause sufficient current flow through the muscles or nerves.

The supernatural current of God can also bring harm as good as it is. This power brings life but when not properly handled, can bring destruction and death.

# CHAPTER 8

## HAZARD SIGNS

*"...He permitted no man to oppress them; And He reproved kings for their sakes: Do not touch anointed ones and do my prophets no harm."* Ps.105:14-15.

*"I will bless those who bless you, and whoever curses you I will curse; and all peoples on earth will be blessed through you."* Gen.12:3.

Genuine Men of God are gifts to mankind but unfortunately a lot of people still do not understand this and consequently have not been able to receive and enjoy these gifts to the maximum.

Ephesians 4:11-13New Life Version (NLV)

11 Christ gave gifts to men. He gave to some the gift to be missionaries, some to be preachers, others to be preachers who go from town to town. He gave others the gift to be church leaders and teachers. 12 These gifts help His people work well for Him. And then the church which is the body of Christ will be made strong. 13 All of us are to be as one in the faith and in knowing the Son of God. We are to be full-grown Christians standing as high and complete as Christ is Himself.

God clearly puts out a hazard sign to warn those who would rough handle his gifts. When you fight a Man of God you are fighting God and no man fights against God and wins. Apostle Paul made a proffession out of persecuting God's people only to find out he had been attacking God all along. Listen from the horse's mouth:

Acts 26:2-18 New Living Translation

2. "I am fortunate, King Agrippa, that you are the one hearing my defense today against all these accusations made by the Jewish leaders, 3. for I know you are an expert on all Jewish customs and controversies. Now please listen to me patiently!

4. "As the Jewish leaders are well aware, I was given a thorough Jewish training from my earliest childhood among my own people and in Jerusalem. 5. If they would admit it, they know that I have been a member of the Pharisees, the strictest sect of our religion. 6. Now I am on trial because of my hope in the fulfillment of God's promise made to our ancestors. 7. In fact, that is why the twelve tribes of Israel zealously worship God night and day, and they share the same hope I have. Yet, Your Majesty, they accuse me for having this hope! 8. Why does it seem incredible to any of you that God can raise the dead?

9. "I used to believe that I ought to do everything I could to oppose the very name of Jesus the Nazarene.a 10. Indeed, I did just that in Jerusalem. Authorized by the leading priests, I caused many believersb there to be sent to prison. And I cast my vote against them when they were condemned to death. 11. Many times I had them punished in the synagogues to get them to curse Jesus.c I was so violently opposed to them that I even chased them down in foreign cities.

12. "One day I was on such a mission to Damascus, armed with the authority and commission of the leading priests. 13. About noon, Your Majesty, as I was on the road, a light from heaven brighter than the sun shone down on me and my companions. 14. We all fell down, and I heard a voice saying to me in Aramaic, 'Saul, Saul, why are you persecuting me? It is useless for you to fight against my will.e'

15. "'Who are you, lord?' I asked.

"And the Lord replied, 'I am Jesus, the one you are persecuting. 16. Now get to your feet! For I have appeared to you to appoint you as my servant and witness. You are to tell the world what you have seen and what I will show you in the future. 17. And I will rescue you from both your own people and the Gentiles. Yes, I am sending you to the Gentiles 18. to open their eyes, so they may turn from darkness to light and from the power of Satan to God. Then they will receive forgiveness for their sins and be given a place among God's people, who are set apart by faith in me.'

After his encounter with God, Paul became blind for three days until a Man of God prayed for him to regain his sight. Please be careful when you deal with the anointing and the anointed because God would come after you. Same way electric currents electrify and electrocute, the sword of God is double edged.

One edge protects, while the other destroys. It all depends on what side you stand. Just as it takes training to handle electricity properly so also it requires training to deal with the anointing of God. It can heal but it can also kill.

## BENSON IDAHOSA AND CHURCH ELDERS

The first instance with Idahosa had to do with four elders in his church led by one Elder Ogolo who were upset that Idahosa embarked on building the 500 capacity auditorium in Iyaro in 1970. According to them, his eyes were too big for daring such a big project since he had only 40 members then. We cannot have a hand in such a foolish project they said. Adamant, Idahosa asked the bricklayers to continue and in reaction, one of the elders went to remove the foundation blocks overnight.

The next day, Idahosa declared "whoever removed these blocks will see this building erected but will not worship here". He then replaced the blocks and proceeded on an assignment in Lagos after choosing Elder Ogolo to stand in from him.

Prompted by the Holy Spirit however, he returned to the church and was informed by his wife that the four elders had taken over the church. "If the Lord wants to raise Elder Ogolo up, He will see that Elder Ogolo remains, but if it is not the Lord's doing, I will take my position.

On sunday morning, Idahosa walked into church and was told to sit down as a member of the congregation. Benson later walked abruptly to the pulpit and preached a message. He ended by saying "We will leave the matter in God's hands and see what happens". Two days later, the chairman of the mutinous meeting died of malaria. The next day, the man who removed the foundation stones lost his daughter.

On the third day, the third elder was rushed to the hospital for tuberculosis and by that Friday, Elder Ogolo was rushed to the hospital with a heart attack and later transferred to Calabar for further treatment. In the end two of the elders and two children died and Idahosa conducted some of the burials. Idahosa's position was vindicated.

## IDAHOSA AND TELE-EVANGELISM IN NIGERIA

In the second instance, Benson Idahosa decided to introduce tele-evangelism in Nigeria. "We cannot allow that" said the female Director to the woman sent by Idahosa. "Only over my dead body will any religious programming be ever put on air."

Benson sent two other people and the woman turned them off saying "Why should we give you special consideration? The Catholics have been here for more than a hundred years and other denominations are older than you. Church of God Missions is just a young organisation which nobody has heard of."

Finally, Benson Idahosa went to see her. "Did you not get my message?" she replied, "only over my dead body will a gospel program go on this station". "No, it won't be over your dead body Madam, you will be alive and you will watch our program but you will never be on television" he replied her.

Three months later there was a shake-up in government and she was dismissed for an infraction. Idahosa approached the new man and immediately he agreed to air the program thus leading the way for every other church on Television today in Nigeria to appear on air.

## PASTOR E.A ADEBOYE AND MR. OBAZEE

Just recently in Nigeria, stories appeared on how a certain Mr Obazee, a former pastor in Redeemed had gone for the jugular of The Leading Pastors in the nation and especially Pastor Adeboye. This is the story of a former pastor of the church who used his headship of a parastatal in the government to oppose the leadership of the church and in particular, his former church.

An ungodly law that all general overseers should resign after a certain number of years, started as an expression of grief by one man, Jim Obazee who became aggrieved by his pastor and general overseer. This man is the now sacked boss of the Financial Reporting Council of Nigeria.

Jim Obazee was a zonal pastor with the RCCG who became envious of the success and power wielded by the General Overseer. He became head of the FRC after repeatedly sending petitions against his boss to whom he was number two to the higher authorities until he had his way.

Jim Obazee, it seemed has been bitter for sometime. He had always spoken ill of his pastor to whoever listened. While he was still a pastor under the RCCG, he bragged that he had not stepped his foot into the Redemption Camp in many years.

He had always complained that the G.O (General Overseer) had asked other pastors to step down after reaching 70 years and he himself has refused to do so which is a matter well captured in the RCCG constitution. He had bragged on a few occasions that he would ensure the G.O steps down.

He disobeyed the G.O in 2012 when the G.O asked that he should see him. Only then was his church file as a pastor reviewed and he got suspended from the church. He outstretched himself when he got someone to introduce him to the then president. There, he found an opportunity to present this matter to the president and gave reasons why churches and mosques should start paying taxes. He convinced the president then by running down God's servants.

This matter was captured in the constitutional conference of 2014.

Jim Obazee was an easy tool then because he came very handy to be used against the then Central Bank governor which led to the governor's suspension from office. This drew him closer to the president and got him the president's ear. It was at that point he made way to express his devilish desire against the church with his G.O as main target.

When the church suspended him and the then president left office, he quickly joined himself to Latter Rain Church and got introduced to the pastor through a member of staff of the FRC who worships there. This he did subtly because of the closeness of the pastor to this present government so he can get introduced to the new President, Buhari. That was done.

His staff in the office all the while groaned under his hard leadership and could not speak out because he had held them bound with threats and fear. This man made himself an enemy of the church and has allegedly been implicated in wizardry and witchcraft and also belonging to the occult. He had some cases of abuse of office and immoral activities going on in court against him which he lost recently.

It seemed his agenda was playing out. He also boasted that it will spread to all the other long serving G.Os and church leaders until 9th January 2017 when he lost his office by Presidential directive.

In all this, the message is clear. Be careful in dealing with men who represent God on earth. Attempts to touch His servants wrongly will have consequences.

*"And now I say unto you, Refrain from these men, and let them alone: for if this counsel or this work be of men, it will come to nought:*

*But if it be of God, ye cannot overthrow it; lest haply ye be found even to fight against God." Acts 5:38-39',*

## BENNY HINN AND KENNETH COPELAND

One day, Kenneth Copeland called Benny Hinn to ask his forgiveness. He spoke against Pastor Benny Hinn in a private meeting with some other pastors in Australia.

While in Australia, he became seriously sick he couldn't minister. While talking to God about his condition, God said to him, "You are sick because you spoke against my servant, Benny!" Immediately, he called Benny and asked his forgiveness.

No man is bigger than the Word of God. Though Kenneth Copeland is a father in the faith, he is still subject to the laws of the anointing.

# "
**You have a right to judge prophecy but don't you ever make the mistake of insulting the prophet.** "

It's okay to judge the anointing but don't insult the anointed.

1 Corinthians 14:29, 6:4-5, 11:31

King Abimelech insulted Abraham, even when Abraham lied, and his entire household fell sick.

Pharaoh tried it with Israel and his whole nation was attacked by plagues and diseases.

Miriam tried it with Moses even when Moses was wrong, and she became sick with leprosy! Don't try God.

# QUESTION AND ANSWERS ON DIVINE HEALING

1 "If someone has the gift of healing, why don't they go and empty out the hospitals?

If healing were entirely in the control of the person who has the gift, then this would be possible. However, the New Testament reveals that healing nearly always involves the faith of the person being prayed for or the faith of a relative or friend. While there are a few noteworthy exceptions in the ministry of Christ worth considering, the vast majority of biblical healings reveal that someone, in addition to Christ, had faith for the healing. As the ministry of Christ is analyzed, there are four clear categories of the kinds of persons Christ healed. There are also two categories of persons not healed in Christ's ministry. These categories explain why a person with the gift of healing cannot empty out a hospital. Here are four categories of those who were healed:

1. There were those who came to Christ on their own and were healed. Their faith was evident by their behavior because they came to Christ for healing. Thousands of people seemed to receive their healing this way. Most often, these people received healing in Christ's mass healing events.

However, some of the specific healings in Christ's ministry also fit this category, such as healing of the woman with the issue of blood[1]. Christ often responded to these people by saying your faith has healed you. This category seems to cover the great majority of Christ's healings and seems to be the most ordinary way to conduct healing ministry.

2. There were those who were brought by someone else to Christ and were healed. In these cases, the faith of someone else was evident by their behavior. Again, thousands of people seemed to receive their healing in this way, and often received healing in Christ's mass healing events. A few specific examples also fit this category, such as the man whose friends lowered him through the roof to Jesus. The account says that Jesus, seeing their faith, healed this man[2]. Together categories 1 and 2 cover the vast majority of healings in Christ's ministry.

3. There were those in need of healing who could not come, but someone else -- a friend or relative -- sought for Christ to come to the needy person. There are a handful of recorded examples in the Gospels of Christ regarding this type of healing. Again, the faith of another person who cared about the sick or injured person was involved in the healing.

Their faith was revealed by their effort to get Christ to come to the person in need. The healing of the Centurion's servant[3] and the healing of the Syrophenian woman's daughter[4] are situations that fit this category. In each of these two situations, Christ gives credit for the healing to the faith of the relative or friend. While this is an ordinary way to heal, it is still a much less frequent way that Christ healed the sick.

4. There were those who did not come at all and Christ seemed to seek them out for healing. There are only a very few examples of this among the thousands of healings and miracles in the ministry of Christ. These healings are extraordinary, and it is important that healing theology acknowledges that they are extraordinary. It seems practical and prudent that the theological foundation for healing be based on the ordinary rather than the extraordinary. One of these examples is found in the Gospel of John, Chapter 5.

The man at the pool at Bethesda had been sick thirty-eight years and Christ initiated the events of this man's healing. In fact, even after the man was healed, he did not know who had healed him. It appears that Christ purposely went to the pool in Jerusalem where there were a great number of sick and injured people.

Christ may have been looking for someone whom He could heal in order to get all the suffering people at this pool to believe in Him as their Healer. After healing this man, it is likely that the good news about this healing reached the ears of many that were seeking healing at Bethesda's pool. It is also possible that many of them sought out healing from Christ in the weeks and months to follow. In this case, Christ was able to use His own faith to produce the healing of this man. Christ seemed to catch this man completely by surprise.

A second example in the ministry of Christ is the resurrection of the widow's son found in Luke 7:11-18. In this account, it appears that Christ has again surprised everyone with this miracle. There is no chance of anyone responding either negatively or positively to Christ in this matter. In these two cases, it appears that Christ's own faith is enough to accomplish the work of the Father, as long as He does not encounter unbelief and doubt among the people He is seeking to serve. Perhaps surprising someone avoids an unbelieving response.

Emptying a hospital would require this type of extraordinary healing repeatedly. Considering Christ's limitations in His own hometown, not even He would be able to accomplish this. This would be similar to the situation at the pool at Bethesda.

The afflicted people at this pool were not seeking Christ as Healer, and He was limited in the help that He could offer. Only this man was healed at that particular time. The vast majority of people in hospitals are not seeking Christ for healing. This is much like the pool at Bethesda. The people at this pool in that story were not seeking healing from Christ. Christ only healed the one man. Any help that a person with healing gifts could offer in a secular hospital under normal conditions would be limited. However, individuals within that hospital setting could be healed like anyone else if they come to Christ for healing.

The other two categories that must be considered are those who were not healed in Christ's ministry.

A. Some were not healed because they did not come to Christ because they did not hear about Him healing. The majority of those who remained ill or injured in Israel were those who did not come to be healed. They did not come simply because they did not hear Good News that Christ is Healer. The same problem remains today. The Gospel is often preached without revealing Christ as Healer. Consequently, many Christian people do not respond in faith to Christ the Healer and struggle on with sickness and injury when healing is available.

B. Some who heard about Christ healing people responded in unbelief and did not come and were not healed. In Christ's own hometown, the people responded in unbelief to Him, and Christ was unable to do much to help the sick and injured there. The implication of unbelief is present in many passages. Christ's critics and persecutors among the religious leaders were certainly unbelieving. Very probably some of these critics and their families were in need of healing but did not come because of unbelief. Although Christ was present and healing was available, most of them were not healed. Today, critics of healing ministry are likely to be in the same situation. Their criticism and unbelief will prevent them from seeking a Christian person equipped to help someone receive healing.

## 2. Doesn't a strong emphasis on faith condemn those who are struggling with sickness?

No. It should not condemn anyone. Anyone can obtain faith for healing. Christ Himself put great emphasis on faith in matters of healing. Anyone wishing to emulate the Savior's supernatural ministry must also teach as He taught. In many of the accounts of His healings, Christ took the opportunity to comment or teach about faith.

Misunderstanding concerning the nature of faith is what creates condemnation. Some have taught faith as if it were a static, unchanging thing. They have improperly taught that either you have faith or you do not have it. However, true faith constantly changes. Faith has to do with our active reliance upon Christ. Faith can grow or decrease in strength. Faith is affected by our understanding of the Father's will. Faith is affected by our theology. Faith is affected by doubts. Faith is affected by the clarity of our revelation of the love of God.

Prayer and diligent Bible study can affect faith as long as we allow the Holy Spirit to use these means to adjust us. Faith for healing often comes to an individual after hearing a bold proclamation of Jesus Christ as Healer. Faith can be released. Faith is not static, but a dynamic reliance upon a faithful Healer. While a person may have been weak in faith yesterday, they may have their faith released today by a faithful presentation of the Gospel. While they may be struggling today, the destruction of a theological doubt, a mental stronghold, can release a brand new experience of healing tomorrow. No one should ever allow the enemy to condemn them as they seek to know Christ as their Healer. The enemy wants them to give up. However, the Father is on their side and will work with them until they are healed.

3. What about people who have strong faith in Christ as Healer and have not been healed?

This is a difficult question to answer because it has an answer that is troublesome to some and offensive to others. The answer can make it seem as if those doing healing ministry are hard-hearted and insensitive to the struggles and suffering of some of God's people. The answer can produce defensiveness and reactions of loyalty in those having genuine compassion for those that are struggling. However, the question must be addressed if theological doubts are going to be completely removed on the matter of healing and help offered to struggling believers. The question itself has several important hidden assumptions that need to be addressed.

First, the question seems to indicate that the unhealed person's faith was unmistakable.

However, experience reveals that these situations are often not what they seem on the surface. Often strong faith of these struggling people is mixed with significant theological doubts and misunderstandings of healing. These doubts can only be discerned and revealed by counseling with these persons. Fortunately, today there are more Christians being equipped to deal with these doubts biblically.

Many times, biblical counseling and working through a sick person's doubts will result in their healing. Christ points out the relationship between faith and doubt in Mark's Gospel.

*Truly I say to you, whoever says to this mountain, 'Be taken up and cast into the sea,' and does not doubt in his heart, but believes that what he says is going to happen, it shall be granted him.* Mark 11:23

This is encouraging. Those who believe that they have faith in Christ as Healer and have not yet received healing need only to seek to remove their doubts. Many times this is the case of those who have not received. They have faith in Christ but their remaining doubts prohibit their receiving.

Secondly, the question also assumes something that cannot be assumed. The question assumes that we can know if another person has faith. Faith is an issue of the heart. No one knows his or her own heart much less the heart of another person. Love, compassion and loyalty sometimes makes us want to assume something about a person that we love that may not be entirely true and cannot be known for sure about another person or even ourselves. It is difficult to be objective about matters that involve us so personally.

Likewise, we are likely to confuse hope, sincerity and possibly even desperation with faith. We are likely to assume that some actions reveal faith such as lengthy passionate prayer and fasting. However, none of these things are faith. They are good works that may or may not be inspired by faith in Christ. Fear and desperation rather than faith may inspire these good works.

Thirdly, the question also presupposes that it is possible to have faith for healing and not be healed. This assumes that the Bible's promises of healing, numerous as they may be, are not reliable as its promises are in other matters. It assumes that the Father is a respecter of persons, doing for one person what He will not for another although the same conditions were met. All of these assumptions are decidedly unscriptural and do weaken faith in Christ as Healer. The assumption that it is possible to have faith for healing and not be healed is full of doubt itself. The doubts that this unscriptural idea produces could be the hidden reason healing has not yet come. God is always faithful to fulfill His promises when the conditions are met.

Fourth, this question invites the blame game. This makes it an unhealthy question. It balances the righteousness of the unhealed person against the righteousness of God.

Either we must blame the unhealed person or we must subtly blame God for not fulfilling His promises. Those who blame God and justify the unhealed person often are blind to their behavior. They generally cannot see that they are blaming God and presenting Him as mysterious, unpredictable and unreliable in healing. This, of course, creates future doubts for everyone affected by this presentation of God. Blaming anyone -- God or the unhealed person -- is unproductive for the Kingdom of God. Let us affirm that God is faithful to His promises and patiently work with unhealed people to receive His grace without resorting to the blame game.

## 4. Doesn't Paul's thorn in the flesh reveal that God was not willing to heal Paul?

Poor teaching about Paul's thorn in the flesh has created doubts in the minds of many people. These doubts have been sufficient to block healing for many people. Therefore, it is necessary to thoroughly analyze this passage. The primary verse in question is found in Paul's Second letter to the Corinthians. This verse reads: *And because of the surpassing greatness of the revelations, for this reason, to keep me from exalting myself, there was given me a thorn in the flesh, a messenger of Satan to buffet me-- to keep me from exalting myself!* 2 Corinthians 12:7

The questions to be considered in analysis of this verse are:

·What is the context of the verse?

·What does the verse actually say that the thorn is?

·What does the Greek word that is translated "thorn" reveal?

Hopefully after these questions are answered honestly, then a good interpretation of this verse will be apparent.

The context of these verses is revealing. At the end of the previous chapter, Paul is relating all the suffering, dangers, beatings, and imprisonment that he endured for the sake of the Gospel. He does not mention sickness. In that context in chapter 11, Paul speaks of being weak but certainly not as a reference to sickness but as a reference to the difficulties that he endured.

At the beginning of chapter 12, Paul begins to explain that he had special revelations of Paradise, of the third heaven. Then he begins to speak of a thorn in the flesh given to keep him from exalting himself as a result of thesurpassing revelations of the third heaven, paradise. Therefore, by implication, a thorn in the flesh is given when someone has special surpassing revelation from God. A truth emerges that should help most people's faith:

Most people would not qualify for a thorn in the flesh no matter what the thorn may be simply because they are not having surpassing revelations of paradise like Paul describes.

Paul says that he asked the Lord three times to remove the thorn but the Lord answered that His grace was sufficient for Paul and thatpower was made perfect in weakness. The Greek word translated weakness is again used. There are a number of Greek words used in the New Testament used exclusively for sickness. This word is not one of them. It was also used a few verses earlier in the previous passage in a context that has to do with persecution. Paul is probably usingweakness again in this way. A verse in the next chapter seems to indicate this strongly. Both words, power and weakness, are also used in this verse. In this verse, Paul says:

*For indeed He (Christ) was crucified because of weakness, yet He lives because of the power of God. For we also are weak in Him, yet we shall live with Him because of the power of God directed toward you.* 2 Corinthians 13:4

Paul is not saying that weakness is sickness. In fact, Paul says that Christ was crucified because of weakness. It puts the term weakness into the context of what unbelieving people were able to do to Christ.

They were able to persecute Him to the point of crucifixion. Paul uses this word in the same way. Paul's weakness was the suffering that he had to endure at the hands of enemies.

The ordinary Greek words exclusively used for sickness in other passages do not appear anywhere in this context. Additionally, just a few verses after writing about the thorn Paul writes that the signs of the apostle were present in his ministry. He mentions signs, wonders and miracles. It is unlikely that Paul would tell his readers about his own sickness and then a few verses later reveal his ability to do miracles. The context reveals that thisweakness, the thorn in the flesh, must be something other than a sickness or a medical condition of some type.

What does the verse actually say that the thorn is? The verse actually does reveal what the thorn is. Paul says that the thorn is a messenger of Satan. The Greek word that is translated messenger is the same word that is often transliterated as angel elsewhere in the New Testament. Paul tells us that the thorn in the flesh is an angel of Satan. It is a leap-of-logic to say that this is sickness. Paul is describing a fallen angel as his thorn in the flesh. Since Paul tells us through the context of all the persecutions he received, a more reasonable interpretation would be that Paul was asking the Lord to stop the actions of a fallen angel who stirred up persecution against Paul wherever he went. In the same way that the devil stirred up trouble leading to the crucifixion of Christ, Paul was suffering trouble caused by this fallen angel. This seems to be validated by further study of the words used in this context.

What does the Greek word that is translated "thorn" reveal? The use of this Greek word reveals a great deal. The Greek word that is translated thorn is skolop. This Greek word only appears in the New Testament in this verse. However, this Greek word appears three times in the Septuagint, the ancient Greek translation of the Old Testament. A great deal of evidence exists that suggests that Paul and other First Century preachers used the Septuagint to preach from throughout the ancient world. The apostle Paul was probably very familiar with how skolop was used in this ancient version of the Old Testament. Skolop is found in three passages in the Septuagint; Numbers 33:55, Ezekiel 28:24 and Hosea 2:6. In Numbers, this word is used in reference to the enemies of Israel.

But if you do not drive out the inhabitants of the land from before you, then it shall come about that those whom you let remain of them will become as pricks in your eyes and as thorns (skolop) in your sides, and they shall trouble you in the land in which you live. Numbers 33:55

This use of skolop above supports the interpretation that Paul's thorn in the flesh had to do with persecution from enemies stirred up by a fallen angel. The passage above does not support the idea that sickness was in some way involved.

The second place where skolop is used is found in the Book of Ezekiel. In that context, God declares that Sidon and other enemies will no longer be a thorn in Israel's side. This usage supports the idea that the thorn has to do with enemies rather than sickness.

*And there will be no more for the house of Israel a prickling brier or a painful thorn (skolop) from any round about them who scorned them; then they will know that I am the Lord GOD. Ezekiel 28:24*

In Hosea, the use of this word is not as clear as the previous two uses. The verse simply says that God will prevent His people from going after false lovers by a wall of thorns.

*Therefore, behold, I will hedge up her way with thorns, (skolop) And I will build a wall against her so that she cannot find her paths. Hosea 2:6*

There are four believers in the New Testament who are often used as examples of believers who were not healed. They are: Timothy had frequent ailments.Epaphroditus was a sick Christian leader at Philippi.Paul left *Tropimus* behind because he was sick.Paul describes a time when he was sick.

We will examine these examples briefly and then comment on how they are being used today. The first of these examples is a verse found in Paul's first letter to Timothy. There Paul writes:

*No longer drink water exclusively, but use a little wine for the sake of your stomach and your frequent ailments.* 1 Timothy 5:23

Some have noted this verse indicated that Timothy had not been healed but actually this verse does not really say that at all. It does not indicate that healing prayer had been ineffective either. It does not indicate that Timothy had any particular problem at the time of the writing of this verse. It does indicate that Timothy had some reoccurring physical issues. Paul was recommending to Timothy a natural preventative measure, a way of staying well. Paul's comments here do not mean that Paul thought his prayers for healing of Timothy were not effective.

This particular use does not reveal anything else to help except that the verse does not reveal skolop as having a connection to sickness. None of the three uses of this word in the Greek Old Testament relate to sickness and two are related to difficulties with enemies.

In summary, a close analysis of this verse does not reveal that Paul had a sickness or injury. The verse itself reveals that an angel of Satan was the problem and the context reveals that difficulties from enemies is the weakness that Paul asks the Lord to remove. Suggestions from other verses that Paul had eye problems, or other conditions such as speech difficulties, are often built upon the assumptions that Paul's thorn in the flesh was a medical condition. However, the biblical foundation for these speculations and theological doubts is very weak. It is unlikely that Paul's thorn in the flesh was a medical condition. We are not saying that Paul never had a medical condition to deal with. We know that he did like any other person. What we can conclude is that Paul could receive healing like any other believer. Paul does not provide an example of someone that God was not willing to heal.

What about the four examples of people not being healed in the New Testament. Don't these prove that God doesn't always heal? No. What these examples prove, if anything, that healing is not automatic or always instantaneous.

Timothy might have been repeatedly healed but the ongoing stress of his life might have caused him to need additional physical help. This is not contradictory. Paul may have thought that preventative measures were wise. For example, someone asks for prayer for blisters on their heels from badly fitting shoes.

We can pray in faith for healing of their wounds and wisely recommend a preventative measure, a new pair of properly fitting shoes without contradiction. The examples may differ but the principle is the same. If we can successfully prevent illness through natural means, then isn't that wiser than seeking healing after we are sick? If we are ill, then we can count on the will of God being healing for us because of what Christ consistently reveals of the Father's will.

The apostle Paul in the book of Philippians writes about Epaphroditus who apparently was sick to the point of death. This is the second of these four examples. Paul writes:

*But I thought it necessary to send to you Epaphroditus, my brother and fellow worker and fellow soldier, who is also your messenger and minister to my need; because he was longing for you all and was distressed because you had heard that he was sick. For indeed he was sick to the point of death, but God had mercy on him, and not on him only but also on me, lest I should have sorrow upon sorrow.*
Philippians 2:25-27

Epaphroditus recovered from this sickness. Paul credits God with his recovery by writing that God had mercy on him. Since the wordmercy is often connected with the healing of individuals in the Gospels, it is evidence that Epaphroditus was healed. In fact, this example is not really of someone who was not healed, but could be an example of someone who was seriously ill for a season before they received healing. These first two examples do beg the question: Does healing from God always have to seem instantaneous and miraculous? We must answer no.

The third of these examples comes from a single verse. This verse reveals that Trophimus had not received healing at the time it was written. Paul writes:

Erastus remained at Corinth, but Trophimus I left sick at Miletus. 2 Timothy 4:20

Of course, the weakness of this verse is that we do not know what happened the next day. This is a snapshot of a moment in time. We have to assume that Paul had prayed for Tropimus without apparent success up to the point of writing this verse. Beyond that, we can only speculate about the details of this situation. We don't know how sick Trophimus was. We don't know how many times Paul prayed for him. We don't know if he quickly recovered from a simple ailment that would not allow him to travel or he had something more serious for a longer period.

We don't know if he simply recovered in a natural way, died, or was miraculously healed. The unknown outcome of this situation makes this situation a questionable one to conclude anything about healing upon with one exception. The one fact that we can glean from this verse is that not everyone that Paul prayed for received healing immediately. This is not a surprise.

Paul reveals in the book of Galatians that because he was ill, he was able to preach the Gospel to the Galatians. This is the fourth example. He writes:

...but you know that it was because of a bodily illness that I preached the gospel to you the first time; and that which was a trial to you in my bodily condition you did not despise or loathe, but you received me as an angel of God, as Christ Jesus Himself. Where then is that sense of blessing you had? For I bear you witness, that if possible, you would have plucked out your eyes and given them to me. Galations 4:13-15

This situation is similar to the previous one with Tropimus. We do not know the specifics of the situation. We do not know what the outcome of this situation was. It does appear that Paul recovered. He might have been healed miraculously. It does not appear that he was healed immediately.

This situation is also a snapshot of a particular moment in time with no details as to what happened afterward. The fact of Paul being ill, even for a season, does not reveal that the will of God was not to heal him. All ideas of that sort are simply speculations and are not based on what Christ reveals of the Father's will. Christ revealed that the Father wants people well.

These four examples are often cited to support the view that God is selective about who He heals. This is a very wrong conclusion from these passages. The right conclusion would be that these believers had not yet received healing. The reasons that they had not received are unclear and unrevealed by the passages. All four seemed to live beyond these recorded events. Even if these examples included someone who had died from sickness, they still would not reveal the will of God for that person.

The perfect will of the Father is not revealed by anyone but Jesus Christ. The Church's individual experience with healing, good or bad, does not reveal the will of the Father. The fact of the early Church's mixed experience with healing being recorded in the New Testament does not change anything. We can build nothing of theological value on the mixed experience of the Church receiving what Christ has done. Some in that day did not receive Christ as Savior either.

. We cannot assume since that is true that this means that it is not God's will to save all. We can only build reliably on Jesus Christ and He reveals that the will of the Father. He reveals this repeatedly by healing everyone in a multitude. He reveals this consistently by never turning anyone away unhealed.

The apostle Paul is the author of all the verses used in these four examples. Paul would have never used these verses in the manner that they are being used. He was not trying to teach believers that God is not willing to heal some people by these examples. He says nothing at all like that in any of these examples. He was not teaching doctrine by telling us about these people. He was simply relating to the Philippians, the Galatians and Timothy personal news about people that they knew.

It is likely that Paul had prayed for healing for each person and of himself. Instead of Paul believing that the will of God was being revealed when people were not instantly healed, he was having a similar experience with healing that many of us have: Not everyone receives healing immediately.Sometimes, healing follows over a period of days or months. Sometimes, more prayer is needed. Sometimes, a crisis of faith erupts in a person and they experience a profound dealing of the Holy Spirit that leads to healing.

Sometimes persistent prayer is what is needed to see a complete healing. Assuming it is not the will of God because someone is not immediately healed makes it impossible to persist in praying in faith.

These four examples are often cited to support the view that God does not always heal. This is a misstatement. More properly, some do not receive healing instantly or may not receive at all. God is still willing that they receive healing even if they don't receive. In two of these situations (Epaphroditus and Paul) the New Testament reveals that these believers did recover. So how can anyone use them as examples of someone not being healed? They were healed although perhaps not instantly. The right conclusion would be that we simply do not know if these other two believers (Timothy and Trophimus) received healing eventually or not. Two of these situations (Timothy and Trophimus) are simply snapshots of a particular moment in time in the life of these believers. We do not know what happened in the hours and days after those verses were written. The assumption that they were not healed is not based on the New Testament and may reveal a theological bias.

Is healing in or through the atonement? Two of the apostles who walked with Christ, Peter and Matthew clearly connect healing with the atonement.

Isaiah Chapter 53 mixes healing verses with atonement for sin verses. In other words, three places in the Bible clearly connect healing with the atonement. Two of these places consist of primary apostolic witness and teaching. The third is from a primary messianic prophetic passage quoted numerous times in the New Testament about Jesus. Some want to balance against this double apostolic and prophetic witness Paul's silence on the subject of healing in the atonement but it doesn't work. The fact that Paul doesn't say anything at all about the subject doesn't seem to be a good argument for or against healing in the atonement. Most, if not all arguments against healing in the atonement are coming out of theology, reasoning and experience rather than the teaching of the apostles found in the New Testament.

It is important to come to the right conclusion on this matter. If healing is in the atonement, then we can always be sure that God desires to heal when we receive Christ as Healer in faith. If healing is only through the atonement, then healing is some sort of add-on given at God's sovereign choice. It should be evident that it would be difficult to ever be sure that God would heal if healing is only through the atonement. If healing is only through the atonement, then consistent, personal faith for healing would be difficult to obtain. It is not enough to believe that God heals.

One must believe that God wishes (wills) for them to be healed. Faith would be based on less than a stable foundation for the one who believes that healing is through the atonement. It would require a personal revelation, some sort of proof, that God wished the person to be well to inspire faith for healing. Otherwise, doubt would always be present and could prevent reception of healing. On the other hand, if healing is in the atonement, then a believer can always be sure that God wishes them to receive healing. The price would already be paid and healing would be received just like salvation is received.

There is much biblical evidence to believe that healing is in the atonement. First of all, two of the Twelve apostles, Matthew and Peter, quote from the Isaiah Chapter 53 passage in their New Testament books. Both apostles connect the passage with healing. The Isaiah Chapter 53 passage is widely accepted to be a description of what Christ would accomplish at the cross. Matthew writes:

*(Christ) healed all who were ill in order that what was spoken though Isaiah the prophet might be fulfilled, saying He Himself took our infirmities and carried away our diseases.* Matthew 8:16-17

This is a quotation from Isaiah 53:4 that Matthew directly connects with Christ healing all the sick in Matthew Chapter 8. Matthew obviously believed that Isaiah's prophecy was being fulfilled by Christ healing the sick. He obviously believed that Isaiah prophecy was also describing physical healing rather than spiritual. The second quotation is from the apostle Peter. Peter writes:

**He Himself bore our sins in His body on the cross, that we might die to sin and live to righteousness, for by His wounds you were healed. 1 Peter 2:24**

Peter quotes from Isaiah 53:5. First of all, Peter connects the work of the cross very closely to healing in actual words of the verse above. Secondly, he quotes from the prophecy of Isaiah about healing that also connects healing with the atoning work of Christ. We conclude without any difficulty at all that both Matthew and Peter believed that healing wasin the atonement. Thirdly, a quick study of the passage in Isaiah Chapter 53 should reveal a few simple linguistic facts. The language of Isaiah Chapter 53 does not lend itself at all to the idea that Isaiah was trying to separate the work of atonement from the work of healing. Only the phrase below separates the two quotes about healing with Matthew's quote just before it and Peter's quote just after it:

But He was pierced through for our transgressions, He was crushed for our iniquities. Isaiah 53:5a

Again, the quote above is between the two quotes from Isaiah Chapter 53 used by Matthew and Peter. This portion of the verse is unmistakably about the atonement. Isaiah is not separating healing from atonement for sin but is mixing them. Just after Peter's quote about healing this phrase is found:

**All of us like sheep have gone astray, each of us has turned to his own way but the LORD has caused the iniquity of us all to fall on Him. Isaiah 53:6**

In other words, every other statement in these verses is about healing or atonement for sin (forgiveness). This is how this part of the Isaiah Chapter 53 passage is constructed:

Verse 4... bore/carried- sickness/pain phrase quoted by Matthew

directly followed by...

Verse 5... pierced-transgression phrase about payment for sin

directly followed by...

Verse 5... wounds-healed phrase in verse 5b quoted by Peter

directly followed by...

Verse 6... iniquity-on Him phrase about payment for sin.

Isaiah's prophecy mixes the ideas Christ paying the price for healing with Christ paying the price for the forgiveness of transgressionand iniquity. To then say that healing is not in the atonement, is an arbitrary statement that is not based on the linguistic facts of this passage. The passage does not separate the ideas. Theology separates healing and forgiveness in the atonement is without biblical license to do so.

Thirdly, the fact that Christ used forms of the Greek word sozo eighteen times where someone is healed is striking evidence that healing is part and parcel of salvation. Other forms of this word are translated as salvation. This was discussed in detail in a previous chapter.

Fourthly, bad logic often plays a part in the decision to believe that healing is not in the atonement but through it. A summary of some of that reasoning is this:

No one who has believed for forgiveness has ever been denied, but multitudes who have believed for physical healing have been denied. Therefore, healing cannot be in the atonement like forgiveness is in the atonement.

This logic sounds convincing but contains many assumptions that cannot be proven. This statement assumes that no one who has believed for forgiveness has ever been denied. While this statement is scriptural and certainly acceptable, it cannot be observed and proven. Neither faith nor forgiveness of sin can be observed or measured in people. Neither can they be proven experientially. They must be assumed by an outside observer. This makes this statement a statement of sincere belief and nothing else. There are some who would contradict it out of their understanding and experience.

Some people think that they have believed but have not received forgiveness. Most of us would immediately reject this as being untrue. We would kindly correct them that they had not believed in a proper biblical way. We would tell them that intellectual assent to the facts of the Bible, desperation, being good, church attendance, and sincerity are not the same thing as saving faith in Christ and if they truly had believed, they would have experienced forgiveness.

The statement that multitudes who have believed for physical healing have been denied is not observable or proven either. It is a statement of belief and nothing else.

Believing on the part of these people cannot be observed either. We cannot know what is in another person's heart and cannot righteously make the judgment that they properly believe in Jesus as Healer and yet are not healed. Many things are confused with faith for healing.

Intellectual assent to the fact that God heals is not the same thing as overcoming faith in Christ as Healer. When someone who appears to believe and has not received healing is interviewed about their beliefs, they often have significant doubts that need to be addressed before they receive healing. A person may appear to believe and even believe that they have faith in Christ as Healer, but this is always an assumption on their part and others. Receiving healing alone proves that they have believed properly in Christ as Healer.

Fifthly, beyond this, when we teach about forgiveness, we teach with conviction that God will always forgive. When the Church teaches about healing this is not the case. The Church often imparts all its doubts and unbelief such as the statement that we are analysing. If the Church taught about forgiveness in similar ways that it teaches about healing, then many would have trouble receiving forgiveness. It is not surprising today that some who theoretically believe in healing have difficulty receiving healing.

If healing were taught with the same assurance that God would heal as easily as He would forgive, then those hearing would receive healing easily. It is not uncommon to see those who have serious theological doubts about healing in the atonement to have problems receiving healing.

Sixthly, there are a few unwise Christian leaders who theoretically believe in healing who do not want to believe that healing is in the atonement. They recognize the significance of this belief. If healing is in the atonement, then God's will is healing in the same that God's will is salvation. These beliefs will put pressure on them to help people receive healing and a few leaders do not want this kind of pressure. Some are afraid of failure. Some of these leaders have told me that they will not try to get anyone healed if it means that they will fail at times to achieve healing for some.

A few leaders would rather that no one is ever healed than for them to fail occasionally to get someone healed. Their fear of failure and concern about their reputation outweighs their concern for the well-being of their people. This is often masked religiously by their concern about disappointing their people. They have developed skills for helping people die with assurance but have little skill at risking themselves to help someone be healed.

Humbling yourself to others when healing doesn't happen as you would wish is actually good for the soul and nothing is lost of reputation when people realize that a leader is doing all he can to do to help. Skills can be developed in this area as well.

Is it possible that the power of suggestion is the cause of what appears to be supernatural Christian healing? Assuming this would be placing a great deal of undeserved faith in the power of suggestion rather in what the Bible reveals about healing. There is no doubt that positive thinking and emotions have a supportive effect on the physical body's ability to heal itself just as negative thinking and emotions have a destructive effect.

Research has shown this is true as well as that which has been described as the placebo effect.Improvement of medical conditions has been shown when someone simply believes that a medication or treatment is helping them even if the "medication" is really a placebo that is not really affecting their condition. Belief seems to reinforce the body's limited ability to heal itself even if that belief is not placed in Christ as Healer.

For a number of important spiritual reasons we do not recommend hypnosis but acknowledge that hypnosis does seem to help some people with pain and addictive and destructive habits.

What hypnosis and the placebo effect are able to accomplish are the limitations of what the power of suggestion is actually able to do. If healing ministry is being accomplished by the power of suggestion then why don't we see secular experts on suggestion healing the seriously ill and seriously injured? We do not see hypnotherapists, psychologists, and psychiatrists healing seriously ill or injured people physically or regularly. On the other hand, these limitations are removed when biblical healing is considered.

Multitudes of seriously ill or injured people worldwide are being healed each year through faith in the name of Jesus Christ. Most of these healings are instantaneous and cannot be explained by the body's natural limited capacity to heal itself. Additionally, some that are unable to believe because they are so seriously ill or injured are being healed because someone else prayed and believed for them. The power of suggestion could not have played at part at all in many healings like these.

Is all supernatural healing from God? No. Supernatural healing that comes from any source that does not acknowledge Jesus Christ as the only Savior, Lord, Deliverer and Healer is not from God. The occult, other world religions and new age sources all would fit into this category. The deceptive power behind these religions is the god of this world, Satan.

The devil will do things through his sincere but mistaken servants that deceptively appear to be good. Since demonic activity is the cause of much sickness, Satan simply removes the sickness temporarily to deceive the unwary. Satan does these things to keep people bound by false religions and beliefs that will not save them eternally.

Are manifestations necessary for healing ministry? No. Simple and uncomplicated faith in Christ as Healer is all that is necessary for healing. Healing can and often does occur without anyone feeling anything. However, manifestations allow the believer and the minister of healing to know that healing has taken place. Manifestations of various types, such as heat or electricity (strong tingling) in the hands of the one praying or in the area of the body needing healing, are an ordinary way that the Holy Spirit communicates with us that healing is occurring. Other manifestations are possible but in our experience are not as common. Manifestations such as falling down (commonly called being slain in the Spirit) or holy laughter are legitimate expressions of the work of the Holy Spirit at times.

However, these manifestations can be counterproductive to mass healing ministry if too many people adjust psychologically to performing these particular manifestations when they feel the presence of the Holy Spirit. Often they will fall down before they are healed or be unable to cooperate with the healing minister if they lose control laughing. When these things happen, often people that could have been healed are not.

Can anyone heal the sick? What if I don't have the gift of healing? Yes. Anyone who is a true believer in Jesus Christ can heal the sick since Christ the Healer is living within them. Some believers might be better equipped and spiritually gifted. Some believers might have more faith than others. Some believers might have more experience. Some believers might have better overall or ongoing results but anyone who believes can heal the sick.

The apostle Paul records in 1 Corinthians 14:1 that we should desire earnestly spiritual gifts. This strongly suggests that we can obtain gifts from God that we don't presently have. Paul reveals in Romans 1:11, 2 Timothy 1:6, and 1 Timothy 4:14 that spiritual gifts can be imparted from a gifted person to someone who is not gifted previously.

Ephesians 4:11-12 says that believers are to be equipped for ministry. So we can expect to become increasingly more gifted than we are presently if we are truly Christ's disciples in heart, word and deed.

Is deliverance ministry necessary for healing ministry? Yes and no. If we are going to have consistent results in healing the sick, then we must understand and practice deliverance ministry. This is simply because some of the sick, injured, or disabled people that they encounter are being afflicted by demons. About one-quarter of the healings in Christ's ministry appear to involve deliverance from evil spirits. We must work through our theological doubts concerning deliverance ministry if we are going to have consistent results in healing ministry. However, since the majority of medical conditions are not being caused by demonic activity, it is possible to accomplish a great deal of healing without practicing and understanding or even believing in deliverance.

**Is the inner healing of the emotions or a revelation of the root causes of sickness needed before physical healing can be obtained?**

No. We must refer to Christ's example. Nowhere in the Gospels do we see Christ making the healing of emotions or the revelation of root causes a prerequisite for physical healing.

He doesn't command the Twelve apostles to make these things a priority either. Christ does heal the brokenhearted but there is not a scriptural reason revealed that would make healing of the emotions or anything else a primary concern before healing of the physical body of sick or injured persons. This idea that inner emotional healing or the root cause must be located first is not reflected in Christ's ministry or the apostles. This doesn't mean that emotional healing will not occur if physical healing is the focus of ministry. God knows all the needs of people.

God heals people and not just conditions. God does not separate these things and make one a prerequisite for another. There may be one exception. Deliverance from evil spirits seems to be a prerequisite for lasting physical healing and emotional healing since some physical sickness and emotional problems is a result of the destructive work of demons.

Is there any opposition between divine healing and medical care? No. The body itself reveals that it is God's will to heal. God has so designed the body that it has its own limited ability to heal itself. When that innate power to heal requires assistance through medicine, herbs, diet, rest or any other natural means, it is within the will of God to obtain that help.

We encourage anyone sick or injured to seek all the medical help that they need in the process of believing in Christ as Healer. This would include following your physician's instructions until healing is completely received. Christ is not limited to the natural or to the supernatural. Christ may use a doctor and a minister of healing together to bring wholeness. The only caution that should be given is where medical care crosses over into supernatural methodology. When caregivers use techniques borrowed from other religions such as Buddhism or Hinduism, this kind of "medical care" should be questioned by the patient. A second opinion should be sought if the technique seems to be occultic, spiritual or supernatural rather than just medical.

What is the relationship between lifestyle and healing? There is an obvious relationship between lifestyle and sickness. One can live in such a way to break down their health. However, lifestyle and healing have a different relationship. Healing can be received because of faith in Christ no matter what the previous lifestyle has been. Forgiveness of sins must be acknowledged as a foundation for the entirety of what God does. However, conscience also plays a part in the matter of faith. If one lives a lifestyle that produces sickness in them, then a guilty conscience makes it more difficult to believe for healing.

Likewise, if a person lives a righteous lifestyle, seeing their life and body as stewardship from God, then the conscience is clear and healing is much easier to receive.

It is generally easier for people who live righteously to receive healing when they need it. This is not because they deserve healing but simply because their conscience is clearer. Healing is a matter of the unmerited favor of God. It is a matter of mercy and grace and cannot be earned. We cannot earn healing by living righteously. Unrighteous living cannot disqualify us for healing either. Healing is available for all because of Christ's sacrifice at the cross, no matter what their previous lifestyle has been. Repentance and the reception of forgiveness will cleanse the conscience of one that has abused their body and allow them to receive healing as well.

Many have understood healing as a gracefrom God but some have failed to see healing as a mercy from God. In the Gospels some received healing from Christ after crying out for mercy. Asking for mercy strongly suggests that the person realized that they were the cause of their own conditions. If they had been unable to change, then they would need mercy. Some teach that if a person doesn't repent of a health damaging lifestyle then God will not heal them. This idea creates faith-destroying doubt.

Many who have health destroying habits are healed in our experience. Sometimes they are delivered completely from the habits, sometimes not. Christ never hesitated to heal anyone because they had a health destroying habit. There had to be people in the multitudes that came to Christ that still had bad health habits. He healed them all.

Christ compared sickness and injury with a farm animal falling into a ditch. The implication was that the animal could not get out of the ditch on its own because the sides were too steep or too slippery. He compared healing with someone lifting the animal out of the ditch. Many people are unable to quit doing the destructive things that ruined their health to begin with. They are in the ditch and can't climb out. Only God can get them out of the ditch. A person, who works too hard, doesn't exercise and eats too much may need healing from conditions caused by this behavior. They may not be able on their own to change their behavior. Christ will still heal them and, if necessary, heal them again and again. God's mercy will still lift them out of the ditch. If they fall into it again, God's mercy will lift them out again.

Christ revealed that the Father is willing to heal all who come to Him no matter how their condition came and no matter how powerless they are to change their behavior. Teaching that God is not willing to heal us until we change our behavior means that many good people will not be able to receive Christ's help out of the ditch. This idea creates serious doubts and makes it difficult for many to receive healing. These doubts need to be captured by what Christ reveals in the multitudes. He heals all who come. He shows mercy to all who need help even if they caused their own problems and still have the same behaviors. Christ's mercyneeds to be exalted repeatedly where this false belief has been present in the past.

You say that God wants people well. What about a sickness leading to death? Death will eventually come to every man and woman. However, death can come without sickness or disability being involved. One can die in their sleep. One can lie down in health in their home and wake up in heaven. Sickness, injury or disability are not prerequisites for death. Death comes to the completely healthy also. There are thousands of relatively healthy people who die each year of unexplained physical causes usually referred to as sudden death syndromes. With those who are elderly, normally speaking the cause of death is attributed to organ failure.

In many of these cases, there was no apparent illness. They just went to bed and woke up in eternity. Sometimes an autopsy does not explain their deaths and only rules out outside causes.

While many wonderful believers may die from sickness, this is not a proof that God wanted to use sickness to bring them to heaven. Healing and health were available in Christ whether they received before their deaths. After the death of a believer, it is certain that they will receive what Christ has provided. The resurrection of believers will also be an eternal healing of their physical bodies. It is simply unfortunate for them and their loved ones that they did not receive healing before their deaths, but it is not tragic in an eternal sense for a believer to die by sickness.

Sometimes a tragic thing occurs after the death of a beloved Christian leader. If he died by sickness, then sometimes other leaders feel the need to protect the reputation of that leader. They may honor that leader in an unhealthy way that is destructive to the faith of others and in a way that the dead leader would never allow if he were living. They may suggest that if that beloved leader could not receive healing then it is clear that God did not wish to heal them.

This, of course, undermines the faith of others that hear this justification of the beloved leader. In turn, other people begin to have trouble receiving healing because they believe that if this beloved leader was not healed, then what hope would have (with all their sins and failures) to receive healing. In actual fact, many of these beloved but sick leaders struggle with theological doubt and the death by sickness of other leaders that they have known.

Our experience is the opposite of what most people would believe. It is generally more difficult for leaders, beloved or otherwise, to receive healing than the ordinary believer. God is not the problem. These beloved leaders are loved by God just as much as everyone else but they do not have an advantage with God. They must receive through simple faith in Christ just like everyone else. These leaders simply have more theological and emotional things to work through than the ordinary believer.

What about curses, unforgiveness and other issues that affect healing? The Holy Spirit may supernaturally reveal other issues that prevent the reception of the grace of Christ in healing. However, it has been our experience that when faith in Christ as Healer is taught and doubts scripturally assaulted and destroyed that the vast majority of people can be healed.

If we place emphasis where Christ placed emphasis, then our results will be more Christ-like in healing. Christ frequently taught about faith and doubt in direct reference to healing. He also taught about unforgiveness several times in His general teaching. He once cursed a fig tree but didn't teach about curses affecting people.

We believe that faith is the primary issue in healing but other matters may also occasionally play a part. In the atmosphere of faith in Christ, the Holy Spirit often deals with these matters by a revelation. Sometimes a "counseling session" may be required to get to the heart of the problem. Sometimes people who quickly lose their healing need this additional kind of ministry. They need to deal with the faith issues but may have another issue to deal with that blocks God's grace to them.

On rare occasions, a season of ministry may be necessary to resolve various issues in a few peoples' lives. With a few sick people there is hidden desire to remain sick because of laziness, irresponsibility or desire to control others. These people will outwardly present to everyone that they want to be well. Inwardly, however, they will have mixed motives and will understand that being sick has its advantages.

Until the hidden desire to be sick is repented of, no healing will take place. These people are often skilled manipulators and deceive practically everyone, even themselves, since their sickness is real. These unfortunate people often get worse until the sickness is more than they can bear and then they repent of wanting to be sick. They often require a great deal of deliverance ministry and teaching in order for them to stay well. In our experience, these people probably are no more than one in a hundred Christians. They require compassionate confrontation and very patient ministry.

If God wants everyone healed, why does He need human beings to accomplish this? God does supernaturally heal people without another human being involved. However, in the Bible, God much more often uses human beings to heal. The question above is probably best answered by posing a similar question. If God wants everyone saved, why does He need human beings to accomplish this? The answer involves God maintaining the free-will of human beings. God could openly reveal Himself, override our wills and save and heal everyone. If God were to use this forceful means beyond the testimony, preaching and prayer of people, then people would not be able to freely choose to believe. They would believe because there would be no other choice.

Faith, hope and love would no longer be the universe's ultimate values but would be replaced by abject terror of God and servitude to avoid the consequences of not serving Him. Our Father has no wish for humanity to relate to Him in this manner. The Father wants people to love Him and to be loved by Him through Jesus Christ. God has, in His wisdom, chosen to work through human beings.

Most in healing ministry admit that they do not get everyone healed. Could this be because it is God's will not to heal some? Christ did not get all the sick people in His own hometown healed either. The reason, however, was not that it was God's will but rather their unbelief. There was others who did not believe in Him, such as the Pharisees and Sadducees, many of which who could have been healed but were not.

The Bible does not support the idea that God's will in healing is always done. After all, the Lord tells us to pray thy will be done on earth as it is in heaven. If God's will were always done, why would we pray in that manner? Additionally, there is no sickness or injury in heaven. Praying that God's will be done on earth as it is in heaven reveals that God's will on Earth is healing of all sickness and injury.

Beyond this, Christ teaches His disciples that persistent militant prayer is necessary to receive an answer in some situations. The will of God in many matters is not automatically received without persistence in prayer. Healing is no exception.

What about God's sovereignty? Doesn't sovereignty mean that God can choose not to heal if He wishes?Occasionally, someone will assert the idea that God's sovereignty means that He does not have to heal even if someone has faith for healing. This is a misuse of this theological idea and is in conflict with what Christ revealed. Christ understood exactly what God's sovereignty actually meant. Christ revealed the Father's sovereignty perfectly in healing. God sovereignty, His kingdom, and His rule were being perfectly expressed by Christ saving, healing and delivering everyone who came in faith.

Most of us would not accept the idea that God would not save someone if they came to Christ with saving faith. In the same way, we must not accept the idea that someone who had faith for healing would not be healed by God's sovereign choice. The belief that God could chose not to heal even if the person had proper faith creates a serious accusation against God.

It makes God unfaithful, arbitrary, unpredictable and untrustworthy. This belief seriously undermines faith in God. We must be able to trust and believe in God. He must be entirely and consistently faithful to His Word. His promises to heal must be firm and unshakable. The example of His Son must reveal His ongoing intentions for us all. Otherwise, we are adrift in life's storms with no place to drop anchor.

Many believers and some leaders who have accepted this misuse of God's sovereignty are adrift like this. They have no firm place to rest. They will have trouble finding faith and capturing doubts when they need healing or in ministry to others. They need to return to a Christ-centered view of the will of God. Christ reveals the Father perfectly and this includes His sovereignty. Christ heals all who come to Him.

Is there a "rule of thumb" to help determine what is the will of God in matters when someone is suffering? Yes. There is a significant principle (beyond Christ's own very clear example) that He revealed that should be used as a rule of thumb. Christ in Matthew 7:11 said:

If you then, being evil, know how to give good gifts to your children, how much more shall your Father who is in Heaven give what is good to those who ask Him.

Christ is inviting us to compare what a normal parent would want for their children with what the Father wants for us. Christ is telling us that our common sense about what is good or bad is reliable in spiritual matters. If we would not do something harmful or bad to our own children, then the Father will not do it to us either.

If we would not injure or make our children ill, then Father will not injure or make us ill either. This principle cuts through complex theological thought that confuses good with evil. If common sense says the circumstance is bad, then our Father is not doing it to us. The Father will save, heal and deliver us through Christ reliably and consistently. This is certainly not mysterious for anyone who really knows our Father. It is because we are greatly loved."

## PERFORMING MIRACLES AND HEALING - DR. ROGER SAPP.

1. Matthew 9:20-22, Mark 5:25-34, Luke 8:43-48
2. Matthew 9:1-8, Mark 2:1-12, Luke 5:17-26
3. Matthew 8:5-13
4. Matthew 15:21-28

## CHAPTER 9

## SUPERNATURAL HEALING MEDICINES

**Is there no medicine in Gilead? Is there no physician there? Why is there no healing for the wounds of my people? New Living Translation (Jeremiah 8:22)**

As I bring this book to a conclusion, let me leave this with you.

The same way doctors administer medicines while treating patients in the natural, God has also made available to us some SUPERNATURAL healing medicines. I will just enumerate some of them.

1. The Blood of Jesus - There is power in the blood of Jesus to save the sinner, heal the sick, and deliver the oppressed. GOD'S WORD® Translation - 1 Peter 2:24

Christ carried our sins in his body on the cross so that freed from our sins, we could live a life that has God's approval. His wounds have healed you.

2. The word of God -

English Standard Version - Psalm 107:20

He sent out his word and healed them, and delivered them from their destruction.

3. The name of Jesus - King James Bible - Philippians 2:10
That at the name of Jesus every knee should bow, of things in heaven, and things in earth, and things under the earth.

4. The Spirit - New Living Translation - Romans 8:11
The Spirit of God, who raised Jesus from the dead, lives in you. And just as God raised Christ Jesus from the dead, he will give life to your mortal bodies by this same Spirit living within you.

5. The power of God -
King James Bible - Luke 4:36
And they were all amazed, and spake among themselves, saying, What a word is this! for with authority and power he commandeth the unclean spirits, and they come out.

6. A merry heart - English Revised Version - Proverbs 17:22
A merry heart is a good medicine: but a broken spirit drieth up the bones.

7. Regenerated spirit - International Standard Version - Proverbs 18:14

A man's spirit can sustain him during his illness, but who can bear a crushed spirit?

8. The Power of Agreement - New Living Translation - Matthew 18:19
"I also tell you this: If two of you agree here on earth concerning anything you ask, my Father in heaven will do it for you.

9. Laying on of hands - Berean Literal Bible - Mark 16:18
and with their hands they will take up serpents; and if they drink anything deadly, it shall never hurt them; they will lay hands upon the sick, and they will be well."

10. There are so many healing medicines that the Lord has made available to us. Our faith in the word of God and in God himself is also a healing medicine. New Living Translation - Matthew 17:20
"You don't have enough faith," Jesus told them. "I tell you the truth, if you had faith even as small as a mustard seed, you could say to this mountain, 'Move from here to there,' and it would move. Nothing would be impossible."

There are healing medicines all over the Word of God but these are the few we can talk about. God has made everything available to us

.

## BRING BACK THE POWER

Pope Gregory was showing Thomas Aquinas all the treasures of the Vatican. The Pope said, "We can no longer say with Peter, silver and gold have I none." "Yes," replied Aquinas. "But no longer can we say in the name of Jesus Christ of Nazareth rise up and walk."

James Brown, credited with inventing soul, funk, and hip-hop was performing in Boston the night Martin Luther King was murdered. He managed to control the crowd. Responding to a comment on the power he was wielding to be able to do that, Brown said, "That's not power. That's influence. Only God has power." Mr. Brown, power belongs to God, but God empowers men to destroy the works of the devil and to do great good on earth.
That's power! **HOW GOD ANOINTED JESUS OF NAZARETH WITH THE HOLY GHOST AND WITH POWER...**

It's interesting that the Greek word for power used in 1 Cor 1:18 is dunamis, the word from which we get our English word dynamo, a generator of electrical power.

I've got 240 volts of electricity coming into my home. If I put my finger in the light socket you'd expect that I might get electrocuted. But I won't, not if I've got the fuse in my pocket. It doesn't matter how many volts are connected up to my house if I've unplugged the fuse. The Cross is like the fuse. If we don't live in the way of the Cross, we remove the fuse from our lives and block the high voltage of the power of God.

To release the power of God we need an uninterrupted connection to the source. We need to be closely identified with the Cross.

Embrace the cross today, where the ultimate price was paid. Repent of your sins, receive THE LORD JESUS CHRIST into your heart, ask God for the gift of the Holy Spirit and begin your journey into power.

Get involved in the healing ministry. The power of God is real. Let's invade our world with the power of God. People are dying everyday. Let's extend the love of God to them through his power.

# NINETY HEALING TEXTS IN THE BIBLE FOR MEDITATION AND CONFESSION

1. "And the Lord will take away from you all sickness, and will afflict you with none of the terrible diseases of Egypt which you have known, but will lay them on all those who hate you." (Deuteronomy 7:15)

2. "So you shall serve the Lord your God, and He will bless your bread and your water. And I will take sickness away from the midst of you. No one shall suffer miscarriage or be barren in your land; I will fulfill the number of your days." (Exodus 23:25)

3. "He sent His word and healed them, and delivered them from their destructions." (Psalm 107:20)

4. "He also brought them out with silver and gold, and there was none feeble among His tribes." (Psalm 105:37)

5. "Bless the Lord, O my soul, and forget not all His benefits: who forgives all your iniquities; who heals all your diseases ..." (Psalm 103:2)

6. "Many are the afflictions of the righteous, but the Lord delivers him out of them all. He guards all his bones; not one of them is broken." (Psalm 34:19)

7. "For I will restore health to you and heal you of your wounds," says the Lord. (Jeremiah 30:17)

8. "O Lord my God, I cried out to You, and You have healed me." (Psalm 30:2)

9. "He heals the brokenhearted and binds up their wounds ... Great is our Lord, and mighty in power ..." (Psalm 147:3)

10. "And my God shall supply all your need according to His riches in glory by Christ Jesus." (Philippians 4:19)

11. "But those who seek the Lord shall not lack any good thing." (Psalm 34:10)

12. "For the Lord is a sun and shield; the Lord will give grace and glory; no good thing will He withhold from those who walk uprightly." (Psalm 84:11)

13. "The thief does not come except to steal, and to kill, and to destroy. I have come that they may have life, and that they may have it more abundantly." (John 10:10)

14. "Jesus Christ is the same yesterday, today, and forever." (Hebrews 13:8)

15. Then Jesus returned in the power of the Spirit to Galilee ... "The Spirit of the Lord is upon Me, because He has anointed Me to preach the gospel to the poor.

He has sent Me to heal the brokenhearted, to preach deliverance to the captives and recovery of sight to the blind, to set at liberty those who are oppressed, to preach the acceptable year of the Lord." (Luke 4:14,18)

16. "... how God anointed Jesus of Nazareth with the Holy Spirit and with power, who went about doing good and healing all who were oppressed by the devil, for God was with Him." (Acts 10:38)

17. "But when Jesus knew it, He withdrew from there; and great multitudes followed Him, and He healed them all." (Matthew 12:15)

18. "And when Jesus went out He saw a great multitude; and He was moved with compassion for them, and healed their sick." (Matthew 14:14)

19. "Now it happened on a certain day, as He was teaching, that there were Pharisees and teachers of the law sitting by, who had come out of every town of Galilee, Judea, and Jerusalem. And the power of the Lord was present to heal them." (Luke 5:17)

20. "And when the men of that place recognized Him, they sent out into all that surrounding region, brought to Him all who were sick, and begged Him that they might only touch the hem of His garment.

And as many as touched it were made perfectly well." (Matthew 14:35)

21. "… who came to hear Him and be healed of their diseases, as well as those who were tormented with unclean spirits. And they were healed. And the whole multitude sought to touch Him, for power went out from Him and healed them all." (Luke 6:17)

22. "But when the multitudes knew it, they followed Him; and He received them and spoke to them about the kingdom of God, and healed those who had need of healing." (Luke 9:11)

23. "When evening had come, they brought to Him many who were demon-possessed. And He cast out the spirits with a word, and healed all who were sick." (Matthew 8:16)

24. "Now Jesus went about all Galilee, teaching in their synagogues, preaching the gospel of the kingdom and healing all kinds of sickness and all kinds of diseases among the people." (Matthew 4:23)

25. And He said to them, "Go into all the world and preach the gospel to every creature. He who believes and is baptized will be saved; but he who does not believe will be condemned.

And these signs will follow those who believe: in My name they will cast out demons; they will speak with new tongues; they will take up serpents; and if they drink anything deadly, it will by no means hurt them; they will lay hands on the sick, and they will recover." (Mark 16:15)

26. "Then He called His twelve disciples together and gave them power and authority over all demons, and to cure diseases." (Luke 9:1)

27. "And He called the twelve to Him, and began to send them out two by two, and gave them power over unclean spirits … And they cast out many demons, and anointed with oil many who were sick, and healed them." (Mark 6:7,13)

28. "And when He had called His twelve disciples to Him, He gave them power over unclean spirits, to cast them out, and to heal all kinds of sickness and all kinds of disease." (Matthew 10:1)

29. "But go rather to the lost sheep of the house of Israel. And as you go, preach saying, 'The kingdom of heaven is at hand.' "Heal the sick, cleanse the lepers, raise the dead, cast out demons. Freely you have received, freely give." (Matthew 10:6)

30. "Now God worked unusual miracles by the hands of Paul, so that even handkerchiefs or aprons were brought from his body to the sick, and the diseases left them and the evil spirits went out of them." (Acts 19:11)

31. "And it happened that the father of Publius lay sick of a fever and dysentery. Paul went in to him and prayed, and he laid hands on him and healed him." (Acts 28:8)

32. "And the multitudes with one accord heeded the things spoken by Philip, hearing and seeing the miracles which he did. For unclean spirits, crying with a loud voice, came out of many who were possessed; and many who were paralyzed and lame were healed." (Acts 8:6)

33. "Therefore they stayed there a long time, speaking boldly in the Lord, who was bearing witness to the word of His grace, granting signs and wonders to be done by their hands." (Acts 14:3)

34. "And I will give you the keys of the kingdom of heaven, and whatever you bind on earth will be bound in heaven, and whatever you loose on earth will be loosed in heaven." (Matthew 16:19)

35. "Now there are diversities of gifts, but the same Spirit. There are differences of ministries, but the same Lord. And there are diversities of activities, but it is the same God who works all in all. But the manifestation of the Spirit is given to each one for the profit of all: For to one is given the word of wisdom through the Spirit, to another the word of knowledge through the same Spirit, to another faith by the same Spirit, to another gifts of healings by the same Spirit, to another the working of miracles, to another prophecy, to another discerning of spirits, to another different kinds of tongues, to another the interpretation of tongues. But one and the same Spirit works all these things, distributing to each one individually as He wills." (1 Corinthians 12:4)

36. "Is anyone among you suffering? Let him pray." (James 5:13)

37. "Is anyone among you sick? Let him call for the elders of the Church, and let them pray over him, anointing him with oil in the name of the Lord. And the prayer of faith will save the sick, and the Lord will raise him up. And if he has committed sins, he will be forgiven." (James 5:14)

38. And it happened that the father of Publius lay sick of a fever and dysentery. Paul went in to him and prayed, and he laid his hands on him and healed him." (Acts 28:8)

39. "The effective, fervent prayer of a righteous man avails much." (James 5:16)

40. "Let us therefore come boldly to the throne of grace, that we may obtain mercy and find grace to help in time of need." (Hebrews 4:16)

41. "Ask, and it will be given to you; seek, and you will find; knock, and it will be opened to you." (Matthew 7:7)

42. "Yet you do not have because you do not ask." (James 4:2)

43. "And there is no one who calls on Your name, who stirs himself up to take hold of You ..." (Isaiah 64:7)

44. "So I sought for a man among them who would make a wall, and stand in the gap before Me on behalf of the land, that I should not destroy it; but I found no one." (Ezekiel 22:30)

45. "He saw that there was no man, and wondered there was no intercessor; therefore His own arm brought salvation for him ..." (Isaiah 59:16)

46. "Therefore He said that He would destroy them, had not Moses His chosen one stood before Him in the breach, to turn away His wrath, lest He destroy them." (Psalm 106:23)

47. "Now faith is the substance of things hoped for, the evidence of things not seen." (Hebrews 11:1)

48. "So then faith comes by hearing, and hearing by the word of God." (Romans 10:17)

49. "But without faith it is impossible to please Him, for he who comes to God must believe that He is, and that He is a rewarder of those who diligently seek Him." (Hebrews 11:6)

50. "For whatever is born of God overcomes the world. And this is the victory that has overcome the world – our faith." (1 John 5:4)

51. "Fight the good fight of faith, lay hold on eternal life ..." (1 Timothy 6:12)

52. ...the blind men came to Him. And Jesus said to them, "Do you believe that I am able to do this?" They said to Him, "Yes, Lord." Then He touched their eyes, saying, "According to your faith let it be to you." And their eyes were opened. (Matthew 9:28)

53. Then Jesus answered and said to her, "O woman, great is your faith! Let it be to you as you desire." And her daughter was healed from that very hour. (Matthew 15:28)

54. ...for she said to herself, "If only I may touch His garment, I shall be made well." But Jesus turned around, and when He saw her He said, "Be of good cheer, daughter; your faith has made you well." (Matthew 9:21)

55. Then Jesus said to the centurion, "Go your way; and as you have believed, so let it be done for you." And his servant was healed that same hour. (Matthew 8:13)

56. And Jesus answered and said to him, "What do you want Me to do for you?" The blind man said to Him, "Rabboni, that I may receive my sight." Then Jesus said to him, "Go your way; your faith has made you well." And immediately he received his sight ... (Mark 10:51)

57. "Therefore I say to you, whatever things you ask when you pray, believe that you receive them, and you will have them." (Mark 11:24)

58. "And Stephen, full of faith and power, did great wonders and signs among the people." (Acts 6:8)

59. "... and the prophets; who through faith subdued kingdoms, worked righteousness, obtained promises, stopped the mouths of lions, quenched the violence of fire, escaped the edge of the sword, out of weakness were made strong, became valiant in battle, turned to flight the armies of the aliens." (Hebrews 11:32)

60. "My God sent His angel and shut the lions' mouth, so that they have not hurt me ... So Daniel was taken up out of the den, and no injury whatever was found on him, because He believed in his God." (Daniel 6:22)

61. "And His name, through faith in His name, has made this man strong ... Yes, the faith which comes through Him has given him this perfect soundness in the presence of you all." (Acts 3:16)

62. "... but the word which they heard did not profit them, not being mixed with faith in those who heard it. For we who have believed do enter that rest ..." (Hebrews 4:2)

63. "So we see that they could not enter in because of unbelief." (Hebrews 3:19)

64. "And He did not do many mighty works there because of their unbelief." (Matthew 13:58)

65. "But your iniquities have separated you from your God; and your sins have hidden His face from you, so that He will not hear." (Isaiah 59:2)

66. "The Lord is far from the wicked, but He hears the prayer of the righteous." (Proverbs 15:29)

67. "For the Lord God is a sun and shield; the Lord will give grace and glory; no good thing will He withhold from those who walk uprightly." (Psalm 84:11)

68. "And whatever we ask we receive from Him, because we keep His commandments and do those things that are pleasing in His sight." (1 John 3:22)

69. "My son, do not forget My law, but let your heart keep My commands; for length of days and long life and peace they will add to you." (Proverbs 3:1)

70. "If you diligently heed the voice of the Lord your God and do what is right in His sight, give ear to His commandments and keep all His statutes, I will put none of the diseases on you which I have brought on the Egyptians. For I am the Lord who heals you." (Exodus 15:26)

71. "A sound heart is life to the body, but envy is rottenness to the bones." (Proverbs 14:30)

72. "Hope deferred makes the heart sick, but when the desire comes, it is a tree of life." (Proverbs 13:12)

73. "A merry heart makes a cheerful countenance, but by sorrow of the heart the spirit is broken." (Proverbs 15:13)

74. "A merry heart does good, like medicine, but a broken spirit dries the bones." (Proverbs 17:22)

75. "Anxiety in the heart of a man causes depression, but a good word makes it glad." (Proverbs 12:25)

76. "There is one who speaks like the piercings of a sword, but the tongue of the wise promotes health." (Proverbs 12:18)

77. "Pleasant words are like a honeycomb, sweetness to the soul and health to the bones." (Proverbs 16:24)

78. "... But You are God, ready to pardon, gracious and merciful, slow to anger, abundant in kindness ..." (Nehemiah 9:17)

79. "The Lord is merciful and gracious, slow to anger, and abounding in mercy." (Psalm 103:8)

80. "But You, O Lord, are a God full of compassion, and gracious, longsuffering and abundant in mercy and truth." (Psalm 86:15)

81. "Return to the Lord your God, for He is gracious and merciful, slow to anger, and of great kindness ..." (Joel 2:13)

82. "The Lord is gracious and full of compassion, slow to anger and great in mercy. The Lord is good to all, and His tender mercies are over all His works." (Psalm 145:8)

83. "The Lord is good; His mercy is everlasting ..." (Psalm 100:5)

84. "For as the heavens are high above the earth, so great is His mercy toward those who fear Him ... But the mercy of the Lord is from everlasting to everlasting on those who fear Him." (Psalm 103:11,17)

85. For with God nothing will be impossible." (Luke 1:37)

86. But He said, "The things which are impossible with men are possible with God." (Luke 18:27)

87. "Now to Him who is able to do exceedingly abundantly above all that we ask or think, according to the power that works in us." (Ephesians 3:20)

88. "And if you are Christ's, then you are Abraham's seed, and heirs according to the promise." (Galatians 3:29)

89. "If you diligently heed the voice of the Lord your God and do what is right in His sight, give ear to His commandments and keep all His statutes, I will put none of the diseases on you which I have brought on the Egyptians. For I am the Lord who heals you." (Exodus 15:26)

90. "1. Who has believed our report? And to whom has the arm of the Lord been revealed? 2 For He shall grow up before Him as a tender plant, And as a root out of dry ground. He has no form or comeliness; And when we see Him, There is no beauty that we should desire Him. 3 He is despised and rejected by men, A Man of sorrows and acquainted with grief. And we hid, as it were, our faces from Him; He was despised, and we did not esteem Him. 4 Surely He has borne our griefs And carried our sorrows; Yet we esteemed Him stricken, Smitten by God, and afflicted. 5 But He was wounded for our transgressions, He was bruised for our iniquities; The chastisement for our peace was upon Him, And by His stripes we are healed. 6 All we like sheep have gone astray; We have turned, every one, to his own way; And the Lord has laid on Him the iniquity of us all.

7 He was oppressed and He was afflicted, Yet He opened not His mouth; He was led as a lamb to the slaughter, And as a sheep before its shearers is silent, So He opened not His mouth. 8 He was taken from prison and from judgment, And who will declare His generation? For He was cut off from the land of the living; For the transgressions of My people He was stricken. 9 And they[a] made His grave with the wicked—But with the rich at His death, Because He had done no violence, Nor was any deceit in His mouth. 10 Yet it pleased the Lord to bruise Him; He has put Him to grief. When You make His soul an offering for sin, He shall see His seed, He shall prolong His days, And the pleasure of the Lord shall prosper in His hand. 11 He shall see the labor of His soul,[b] and be satisfied. By His knowledge My righteous Servant shall justify many, For He shall bear their iniquities. 12 Therefore I will divide Him a portion with the great, And He shall divide the spoil with the strong, Because He poured out His soul unto death, And He was numbered with the transgressors, And He bore the sin of many, And made intercession for the transgressors." Isaiah 53:1-12.

The Lord bless you, The Lord increase you on every side and may God's healing current flow through you in the name of Jesus. May The Lord use you mightily in this generation as a generator and a distributor of His healing current.

My name is CMD LAMAI and I approve this message. Thank you and God bless you.

## OTHER BOOKS BY C.M-D LAMAI

1. Joseph The Caretaker
2. Healing Current
3. It's Your Turn
4. Favour Thou Art Loosed
5. The Real Broken

## MINISTRY INFORMATION

To contact C.M-D Ministries about speaking in conferences, salvation, healing and miracle crusades, outreaches, revival meetings and church services or for partnership and testimonies:
E-mail: cmdlamai@gmail.com, cottagechristian@yahoo.com
Website: www.christian-cottage.org
Mailing Address:
Dyersburg Christian Center
Dyersburg, TN, 38024
United States of America

E-mail: cmdlamai@gmail.com
ndamarvel@yahoo.com
cottagechristian@yahoo.com
AFRICA: +234 80515 333 43
U.K: +44 79564 11752
USA: +190 1236 1659

# C.M-D LAMAI

**CMD Lamai** is a lover of Jesus who strongly believes in the supernatural power of God.

He is first a healing priest, known to operate a very unique healing grace for instant healings and miracles, also a conference speaker and pastor.

He is the president of CMD Global Outreach, actively involved in rural, urban and international outreaches like Mighty Miracles in America and Healing Current. He is the Prime Minister of a network of churches worldwide.

CMD Lamai also presides over the March of Faith Int'l Fellowship, Nigeria, with its headquarters in Memphis, Tennessee, USA.

He studied Philosophy, Theology and The Liturgy of the Word from St. Paul's Catholic Seminary, Benin City and holds a Bachelor of Arts degree in Communication and Language Arts from the University of Ibadan and a Masters Degree in Law from the University of South Wales, United Kingdom.

A broadcaster by training, an author of several books by inspiration and a preacher by divine election. His teaching and healing ministries touch lives around Africa, Europe, Britain and America.

His is married to Nike Lamai who pastors with him and presides over a flourishing foundation called, Hadassah Healing Foundation, a ministry that convenes Stadium sized convocations and brings healing to hurting women around Africa, Europe, America and Asia.

Made in the USA
Coppell, TX
30 September 2022

83870977R00108